Growth Mindset:
A Practical Guide

For Finn. Strength and grit has driven us forward. Together.

Growth Mindset:
A Practical Guide

Nikki Willis

BLOOMSBURY EDUCATION

LONDON   OXFORD   NEW YORK   NEW DELHI   SYDNEY

BLOOMSBURY EDUCATION
Bloomsbury Publishing Plc
50 Bedford Square, London, WC1B 3DP, UK

BLOOMSBURY, BLOOMSBURY EDUCATION and the Diana logo are trademarks of
Bloomsbury Publishing Plc

First published in Great Britain by Bloomsbury Publishing Plc

A catalogue record for this book is available from the British Library

ISBN: PB: 978-1-4729-5506-7; ePDF: 978-1-4729-5507-4; ePub: 978-1-4729-5508-1

2 4 6 8 10 9 7 5 3 1

Typeset by Newgen KnowledgeWorks Pvt. Ltd., Chennai, India
Printed and bound in Great Britain by CPI Group (UK) Ltd, Croydon CR0 4YY

To find out more about our authors and books visit www.bloomsbury.com
and sign up for our newsletter

Contents

Introduction
More than a display. Learners for life.

In today's world, children are unlikely to have a job for life – job security is not guaranteed, and competition is high. There has never been a greater need for resilience, determination and effort to produce the results that individuals would like. This is where the growth mindset comes in. A culture that encourages and teaches a growth mindset equips children with skills for life – not only will these skills be valuable in higher education and the workplace, but they encourage individuals to become lifelong learners. A growth mindset teaches children to take personal responsibility for their successes and to understand the impact that their own efforts, resilience and learning behaviours have upon this. A lot has been written about the growth mindset over the last few years. Most schools have acknowledged that it is a fundamental part of helping children become learners for life and to fulfil their learning potential. There is also research that suggests because a growth mindset culture emphasises the importance of mindfulness, self-appreciation and self-esteem, children are generally happier. However, in an education system where many practitioners already feel overloaded with work, it can feel like implementing a growth mindset is just another item to add to an already long to-do list.

This book offers practical suggestions that can help you to gradually create a growth mindset culture in your school. The focus is on enhancing the good work that is already being done in schools without adding to teachers' workloads. In a school with an effective growth mindset culture, children should be eager to learn and should want to achieve – I have always believed that the best lessons are those where the children are working harder than the teacher. It's important to remember that transforming the learning culture of your school will not happen overnight and you will come up against resistance from both children and staff. But, with effective leadership and consistent practice, you will get there. So, let's start at the beginning.

Where did the growth mindset idea come from?

The term growth mindset was originally introduced by Carol Dweck. Dweck has written extensively about the growth mindset and I would highly recommend you read some of her work if you want to learn more about her philosophy (see 'Bibliography' at the back of this book). But, as this is intended to be a practical guide, here is an overview of Dweck's ideas to get you started.

Dweck began her research over 30 years ago. Initially her project was concerned with how children dealt with failure at school. Dweck and her colleagues had observed that whilst some children saw failure as a learning opportunity, many were devastated and demotivated by the smallest setback. Dweck wanted to find out more about how and why students develop these different learning behaviours.

After extensive field research, she concluded that children's learning behaviours are dependent upon their underlying mindset and beliefs about talent and ability. According to Dweck, there are two polarised mindsets: she calls these the fixed mindset and the growth mindset. A mindset is a way of thinking. Individuals with a fixed mindset believe that intelligence and talents are attributes we are born with. They believe that these attributes are fixed, therefore individual effort has a limited impact upon them. In contrast, a person with a growth mindset is someone who believes that intelligence, ability and talent can change and develop if you work hard and challenge yourself. Dweck argues that children with a growth mindset are more likely to fulfil their learning potential and to enjoy the process of learning.

However, Dweck explains that in order for a growth mindset to be effective, it has to become part of an individual's belief system. Beliefs come from repetition and exposure. To ensure that the thoughts and messages of the growth mindset – such as, challenges help us to grow – become beliefs, they have to be practised consistently.

What does the profile of someone with a growth mindset look like?

- They believe effort is the route to full understanding and competence.
- They see challenges as positive steps in learning and so they seek them out. They push themselves to create opportunities to try new things, even if there is a chance they may fail.
- They welcome feedback because they understand that it can help learning and growth.
- Although they might not always view their mistakes as a good thing, they do not see them as 'bad' or an indication of failure – they understand that they can be learnt from.
- They are persistent in the face of obstacles and continue to try.
- They are willing to have a go at tasks without always being worried about succeeding or failing. They understand that you cannot grow if you do not try new things.
- They see reflection as a step towards growth. They know that understanding what went wrong or was successful and how that outcome was reached will enable them to improve next time.
- They are resilient – they can bounce back from mistakes or failures and can appreciate that there are learning opportunities at every stage of a process.

Does this sound like the children in your school? It is unlikely that all children will have this mindset already and even those that do are unlikely to have every single habit in this list. But, by introducing some of the strategies provided in this book, these habits could become more common and more importantly, part of the learning culture in your school.

How did my interest in learning cultures and the growth mindset develop?

In my teaching career I have taken a number of different roles in primary school. I formally worked as a deputy head and an Early Years teacher, with lots of other roles in-between. My job was exhausting but I loved it; I love teaching and seeing children grow. Due to the nature of my role, I was able to regularly observe all year groups in the school. I began to notice that a high number of children lacked any lust for learning – they were disengaged, switched off and they saw 'getting it wrong' as a disaster. I observed children who wouldn't write at length, children who wouldn't try when they were struggling, and I also observed bright children who could coast through lessons because they found everything easy. I knew that there was something wrong. It seemed that the school had created a culture where success was recognised, but anything in-between went unnoticed.

I was concerned about our environment for learning, so I began to research learning mindsets. After learning more about growth mindset, I decided to conduct further research to try to understand how we could develop our school community to ensure that we equipped children with good learning attitudes. I wanted children to have a thirst for learning, be willing to be challenged and be able to push themselves, as well as recognising what can be learnt from failures. With the help of my colleagues, I developed a plan with strategies to help put this vision into place (including Reach for the Stars, which will be covered in more detail in Chapter 2). I led the process initially, but gradually other members of staff and the school community began to see the impact that the growth mindset approach had upon children and so started to take leads themselves. It took three years to fully implement a growth mindset culture in my school and it is still an ongoing project. If you are leading a growth mindset in your school, just keep going because you will get there. It takes time to change a learning culture and even once a new culture is embedded it will still need constant reinforcement, but I know you can do it!

How do you create a growth mindset culture?

Initiating and sustaining an effective growth mindset culture is not simple. In many schools it has been implemented incorrectly and has even become a dangerous term: it has been used to justify amazing displays that tell children they can be anything they want to be and that, if they don't give up, they can achieve anything. But, can they really? Of course, growth mindset theories have some fantastic elements and, if used effectively, they can have real impact, but to do this it is crucial that, as a school, you decide what kind of learners you want your children to be.

An effective implementation of a growth mindset means children understand what learning behaviours are the most effective. Resilience, self-motivation and determination are key learning behaviours that, if developed well in childhood, will support a lifetime of learning. So, put away your motivational quotes and look at what opportunities the children are given to practise these learning behaviours.

Let's put this into perspective with a quick example. Many schools across the country are working hard to raise standards in writing, especially for boys. It has been identified that many learners are scared of failure when it comes to writing because there are so many components that they need to remember to be successful (e.g. spelling, grammar, punctuation, comprehension). They are unlikely to get all of these things right every time, which means that mistakes are frequent. As a result, many children give up quickly. Developing children's learning attitudes so that they understand the value of mistakes will build resilience and give them the confidence to try even if it is not 'perfect'. Later in the book you will find activities that explicitly teach children the skills of using feedback effectively (see Austin's Butterfly on p. 28).

It starts with you

As I already mentioned, you might well experience resistance if you are leading the initiation of a growth mindset. Therefore, you will need to be resilient and determined. To do this you need to start by adjusting your own mindset. Your mindset and how you model it to the wider school community is fundamental to the success of a growth mindset culture. So, before we get stuck in to the practical advice, ask yourself the following questions:

- Considering the definitions given in this chapter, as an individual what is my mindset? Is it growth or fixed?
- How do I manage mistakes?
- What do I model to my colleagues when things go wrong? How do I approach it?
- How would my colleagues describe me as a learner?

Your answers to these questions will help you to identify the strengths and weaknesses of your own mindset and how you need to adapt in order to develop a new learning culture. To introduce and model a growth mindset, you must show that you have one yourself. It is also important to remind your team what their motivation is. In turn, this will help them want to improve the learning environment. The children should be working harder than the teachers!

Getting your team on board

Changing the attitude of a team of adults in a school can be tricky. It is important that they understand the reasons behind the growth mindset for themselves. Let them know how it can change their classroom environment so that children work harder and how this will positively impact results and outcomes. Help them to see the impact it has by allowing them time to observe the subtle changes in learning behaviours. Explain that, as teachers, it isn't actually possible to know exactly what a child's capability is – we make assessments that give us a picture of what their understanding of a subject is at a particular point in time, but it is impossible to ever know a child's true potential. Getting your team to understand this and that part of their role is to help children to fulfil their potential using different strategies is instrumental in creating individuals who want to learn.

Almost all the teachers I have ever met want the best for the children they are teaching. They are enthusiastic souls who can do wonders with a paper plate and can give you a visual way of teaching fractions in a heartbeat. In your school, you will invariably have a range of teaching styles and a range of mindsets, but if a key part of your team culture is that teachers want the best progress in learning, your role as a leader is to model how a growth mindset culture will enable this further.

Lead by example. Ask yourself as a leader: am I promoting a growth mindset in this school? Do my teachers have a growth mindset? If not, how am I helping them to achieve a new way of thinking? How am I modelling that a growth mindset will accelerate the progress in learning in their classroom and in the school as a whole? Start by talking to your team, but try and do it without saying something like, 'We've got something new to talk about and it is going to take a whole INSET …'. Think about introducing some new ways of changing their thinking.

Staff meetings

Staff meetings are regular events in school and often involve an elephant stampede to get caffeine and are surrounded by left-over school dinners. In so many schools, time is wasted in staff meetings on discussions about events and dates. They are often a nuisance to staff who would rather be setting up for the day or spending the time marking. I am not suggesting that you don't need staff meetings – they are useful, but they need to be an efficient use of time. Ask yourself: do they need to be weekly? Are we using this time efficiently to grow and give our teachers the time they need to evaluate and reflect or is it just an opportunity to dish out information that could be distributed in other ways?

At my school a staff meeting was held every Tuesday from 3.30pm. A rushed agenda was sometimes issued, but more often than not there wasn't an agenda at all. 'Dates for the diary' was always high on the list of priorities, which meant that often more time was spent on these than was needed. SLT found it difficult to fit everything in to staff meetings that needed to be covered (e.g. subject leaders, CPD, new schemes). So, a new model was introduced – staff meetings only took place if there was a clear agenda and this agenda was displayed for the team to see throughout the week. We also introduced the HACKS on the next page. Staff breathed a sigh of relief when they realised that they didn't have to listen to a long list of 'information'. We then remodelled staff meetings to include time spent on developing growth mindset, which was done through a focused 30-minute workshop – this allowed staff time to learn, grow and reflect on the culture and the high expectations of the model being implemented. The short workshop session also allowed time for other items to be discussed, if needed, and turned the focus onto staff wellbeing. This meant that teachers were no longer stressed during meetings thinking, 'I could be doing so much with this time'. One teacher said that instead, 'Staff meetings feel like they are a productive use of time and I know feel I am reflecting on my practice'.

Staff meeting HACKS

- Display dates for the diary centrally in the staffroom, rather than discussing them in meetings. Allow the team the ability to make comments in a different coloured pen if they notice any overlaps.

- Assign subject leaders their own notice boards in the staffroom. They can write directly onto it any messages or information they want staff to have. Schedule termly subject leader meetings for a review if needed. Staff to sign with a clear timeline to say they have read and taken actions if required.

- Include pastoral issues, such as concerns regarding individual children, in the morning briefing. This should run from about 8.30am for ten minutes – I would recommend using a timer to ensure it is only ten minutes, so that everyone can get on with their day (or get to the photocopier).

- Make sure there is a clear objective for staff meeting time – even if it's that there will be no meeting. Staff can choose when they do things, but if they know they have been given time they will feel valued.

If staff meetings are managed in a better way and time is used more efficiently, this allows time for staff to work on developing a growth mindset. At my school we have approximately five meetings a term that are an hour in length. Apart from that, communications are put on the large whiteboard in the staffroom and the above HACKS are used. Every week on the planner an objective is set for this time, even if we have chosen not to meet.

How can this book help?

Each chapter offers some practical ways to encourage a growth mindset in your school environment. Here is a summary of what is covered in each chapter.

Chapter 1: Characteristics of Effective Learning – why stop in the Early Years?

It is recognised that the Characteristics of Effective Learning in the Early Years curriculum is fundamental to helping children develop an active eagerness to engage in learning. This chapter explains why these characteristics should be developed across your school to facilitate learners' opportunities to explore and grow and shows you how you can incorporate them in your planning.

Chapter 2: Reach for the Stars – differentiation with a difference

This is a practical resource that will put children in control of their own challenge and help achieve mastery of a lesson. It is all about promoting independence, creativity and giving learners an opportunity to explore their own potential.

Chapter 3: 'I sit with the thick kids who are just like me'

This chapter is all about exploring the classroom environment and the labels we give to children. It includes practical suggestions that do not disregard ability but do challenge the keeping-learners-in-boxes method.

Chapter 4: Independent learning – why should I do it myself?

In order for children to embrace a growth mindset they need to take control of their own learning. To do this you need to encourage them to make their own decisions without being spoon-fed. This chapter offers practical suggestions on how this works in the classroom and in the wider school community.

Chapter 5: Assemblies – a time to learn

Assemblies are an opportunity to get the whole school community together for a common goal. This chapter offers a series of ideas and starting points for holding assemblies that discretely communicate the messages of a growth mindset.

Chapter 6: Another motivational quote? Effective displays

If used well, displays are a powerful tool in schools. This chapter explores working walls and gives ideas for displays that support your new culture.

Chapter 7: Adult talk – why our language matters

In order for a culture to stick, all stakeholders need to be in agreement and understand their role in communicating the message. This chapter covers how to effectively train and support LSAs, as well as how to encourage all adults, governors and office staff to support the learning ethos of the setting.

Chapter 8: The power of the parent

The messages you are promoting in school may be strong, but they will have more impact if you can get parents to understand the growth mindset message too. This chapter covers workshops, communication and practical ideas on how to help them to help you spread the word.

Chapter 9: Impact – what does it look like now?

Measuring the impact is something we hear a lot in education, however it is difficult to see this in some areas of learning. How can you measure the culture and the improvement of growth mindset attitude amongst your learners and adults? This chapter includes practical observation techniques, questionnaires and how to continue to embed the new culture.

Before you start...

As you read this book you will begin to unpick your own school culture. The last chapter asks you to reflect on how your culture has changed and the impact you have had. In order to do this, it is important to make some useful evaluations about what your school culture looks like before you get started. By recording a snapshot before you start, you will be able to look back and fully see the progress you have made in developing a growth mindset for learning.

Here are some quick and easy ways you can do this:

Select a focus group of pupils

Choose approximately ten children from across the year groups. Ask them to complete a simple growth mindset questionnaire. There are many questionnaires available online or you can design your own based on the specific areas you want to focus on. If you are looking online, you can find a good one on this website: https://survey.perts.net/share/toi.

Record your learning walk with SLT

Make notes about what you observe in your learning culture while on learning walks. Date these notes so you can compare your observations at regular intervals once you have started implementing the growth mindset culture. Here are some useful starting point statements for your learning walk:

- Children are very engaged in learning
- Children make their own choices about learning
- Growth mindset language is used regularly
- Feedback is welcomed and useful
- The school is interactive and welcomes views of all
- Children feel empowered.

Ask your staff

It is important to record what your staff mindset is before you get started, so you can reflect on the impact that you have had on them too. Ask them some simple questions – you can do this in a staff meeting or by giving them a questionnaire. Sharing these questions with your team in the staffroom or more publically in the school means everyone understands what you are trying to achieve.

Some examples of questions you could ask are:

- How independent are our learners?
- How child-led is the learning?
- How resilient are our learners?
- How much do our children know about how to learn? The process?

After you've assessed where you are now, you're ready to start your journey towards establishing an effective growth mindset culture in your school. Let's get started!

Chapter 1

Characteristics of Effective Learning – why stop in the Early Years?

Up until three years ago, I taught Year 6. So, when I started teaching in the Early Years it was a massive culture shock but I can honestly say that I loved it. It is in the Early Years that you first get the opportunity to instil a love of learning in those you teach. Central to the Early Years curriculum is the Characteristics of Effective Learning (CoEL). In outstanding Early Years settings, practitioners work hard to provide opportunities to allow children to develop the skills and good learning attitudes that will help them to become independent learners. There is provision for the CoEL in every part of the Early Years curriculum, from early number and literacy development to outdoor learning. Whilst the principles of the CoEL are usually a high focus in Early Years settings, sadly these messages about good learning attitudes are not always followed through into other primary year groups. The CoEL has many of the traits we want to see in our learners in a growth mindset culture – so, why aren't they a focus throughout the whole school?

This chapter gives practical suggestions on how you can further develop the fundamental skills that have been introduced in the Early Years. Rather than the Early Years CoEL being an isolated approach, this chapter demonstrates how schools can use this framework to develop a growth mindset culture throughout all year groups and highlights the importance of these traits at every stage of school life. First, I will explore what the CoEL are and how they are useful. Then, I will give some practical ideas on how you can give children opportunities to continue to explore the CoEL both in and beyond the Early Years.

Development Matters (2017)

Development Matters is a document used by many settings to maintain a high standard of CoEL development. The document is centred on the importance of understanding and providing a curriculum in the Early Years that reflects this:

Unique learner + positive relationships + enabling environment = learning and development.

Using this formula alongside CoEL enables learners to thrive. As an Early Years practitioner, I quickly saw how this structure corresponded to the skills required to develop a growth mindset. In a high-quality Early Years setting, where the CoEL are actively encouraged, children's ideas are valued. This creates fantastic engagement: children are interested in what they are doing and are given some freedom to explore their own ideas and develop their skills.

Characteristics of Effective Learning

Playing and exploring – engagement

- Finding out and exploring
- Playing with what they know
- Being willing to 'have a go'

Active learning – motivation

- Being involved and concentrating
- Keeping trying
- Enjoying what they set out to do

Creating and thinking critically – thinking

- Having their own ideas
- Making links
- Choosing ways to do things

In my opinion, the CoEL messages should be promoted throughout school and used to encourage children to be independent and to want to discover, explore and challenge themselves. As you can see above, the CoEL include some of the most important traits that are necessary to have a growth mindset. In a good Reception setting the CoEL are embedded within the curriculum on a daily basis. However, I have often observed children who leave Reception willing to 'have a go' showing resilience and having their own ideas only to arrive in Year 1 to find they are given a worksheet that forces them to abandon their independent learning. When you walk into a classroom you should be able to see that children are leading the learning and have made some decisions about their own learning journey.

What signs suggest that learning is child-led?

- **Displays**: Have the children contributed to displays or are they just wallpaper printouts? Is the learning on display varied? Does it show individual children with individual ideas? If a display is made up of the same picture duplicated 30 times, how much scope has the learner had to explore their own ideas or interests?

- **Lessons focus on skills rather than knowledge**: When you talk to children, can they explain how they are doing something or are they just regurgitating the facts? For example, I once spoke to children about an electricity experiment they were planning. They spoke about how they could test their theory and how they could use different materials. They were leading their learning with skills first and foremost.

- **Individual approaches to tasks:** Allow children to lead learning. This allows for an individual approach and better engagement.

Consider the following example in light of these questions.

A child is excited to show their teacher the rocket he has made. He explains in some detail that he had decided to make a rocket so that his LEGO® man would be able to go into space. First, he looked in a book at pictures of rockets and then drew a plan of the rocket he wanted to make. He tells his teacher, 'I made a list of things I need – strong glue is important'.

The teacher looks at his list and helps him find the resources he needs, including the strong glue. In this situation the child is leading his own learning – he has written a list, drawn, improved and made his model. He is fully engaged in the process and the skills he is learning and mastering. The adult's role is to expand his thinking even further – this means not just praising the learning but asking questions that open up more possibilities to improve his learning further.

As this example shows, child-led learning is key to outstanding learning. Allow children to choose their interests and then, as practitioners, facilitate the investigation of these interests. This results in a high level of engagement where the learners make decisions about their own learning through the choice of their resources or interests.

Child development and self-image

When a child is in the Early Years, the messages they get about themselves help them to build up an image of who they are. This includes messages they receive from their parents and, of course, from practitioners in nursery and Early Years settings. Major child development theorists such as Dewey, Montesorri and Erikson have all written that children need to be independent to learn, which means that the curriculum needs to be based on their real interests. Understanding how a child learns most effectively is key to providing a stimulating and growth mindset environment. The more a child practises a skill independently and learns from their own interests, the more they will engage with the learning process and hopefully become learners for life. The following activities are used in my school to help promote children's self-image in the Early Years. They can also be carried out in the first years at primary school.

Activities

Developing independent ideas: *The Dot* by Peter H. Reynolds

The Dot by Peter H. Reynolds is a great starting point for getting children to explore their own ideas and think about their own learning processes. It is a great springboard for lots of different activities.

Here are some you could try:

- Read the story with the children and ask them if they can remember a time when they have thought an idea they had was not good enough. Have they ever drawn a picture and thought it wasn't the right thing? Ask the children to reflect and talk about these ideas.

- Draw a dot on the board. Ask children, what do they see the dot becoming? Ask the children to create a dot of their own on a whiteboard – what could their dot be? Using a whiteboard means they can wipe out their drawing if they get a better idea or their idea develops – encourage and model this.

- Hold an assembly where each adult in the school has produced a picture from a dot. Ask children if they can match the ideas to the teacher. They probably will not be able to – this shows that everyone has different ideas and that no one is wrong.

- Run a lesson where each child is given a printed dot and ask them to create their picture. What will their dot be? At the end of the lesson create a gallery. Let the children give feedback on their pictures.

- Create a display in the school of dot pictures. Make sure the book *The Dot* is available for everyone to borrow, read and make comments on. This project can be used as a seed to encourage children to see that we all have own ideas and can explore them. There isn't a set right answer to anything, so trust your ideas and processes.

Display the outcomes from *The Dot* activities

Exploring the story of *The Dot* in the classroom

Building self-image: Special friend

This activity works best if it is carried out over a week. On Monday choose a child and ask the rest of the class to write a compliment about that child – something they like about them or something they have done which has impressed them. Display these compliments in the classroom throughout the week. Take a special interest in that child's learning achievements that week and take photos of examples of work where they have put in lots of effort, shown resilience, bounced back after a mistake or redrafted and improved learning. On Friday read out all the special friend notes and make comments on their achievements in the week. Put them into a special book for the child to take home.

Build a curriculum around children's interests: Let's talk camera

Invest in a camera for your setting and give the children the opportunity to take it home on a Friday. (You may want to laminate some instructions to go with it.) Ask them to take four pictures of things that they love. Set up an area of the classroom where you can display the photos for a week. This will stimulate conversation for the children and is a great self-confidence boost for the 'camera child'. You might like to include prompt questions for other children to ask the child who took the photos. I have seen this simple idea transform the communication of individual children because it gives them the confidence to talk about their own interests. As a teacher, it also gives you an insight into their lives and what makes them excited and interested. On one occasion doing this in my own classroom, a boy took pictures of tractors and dustcarts. Having looked at the pictures, I was able to engage him in the next area of learning using these ideas – I gave him the opportunity to design a supersonic dustcart, which he loved!

Adapt your planning as you go: The planning board

A planning board is a fantastic asset to any classroom. It may include planning for the following week, ideas for provision, photos of successful activities and a timetable for all adults to feel empowered to contribute. It should also highlight gaps in children's learning and how the environment could address these. Observations of the children should be recorded and noted and acted upon. The planning board is a place for all adults to note their observations, for example: Ramil still isn't using capital letters properly – how can we address this next week?

The planning board – make it available for everyone to contribute ideas to

This sounds like an obvious activity, but it is such a great way to encourage adults to listen to the children as they learn. A planning board could have the week's timetable on, objectives, photos and availability for all adults to add notes about how to engage children and their observations. I have seen whiteboards stuck on the planning board so that observations can be regularly written up and changed. This is a very effective and low maintenance way of adding observations and notes. Pose questions to your staff and encourage them to write their answers on the board. What are the children talking about this? What interests them? What's going on outside school at the moment that we can incorporate into learning? In a Year 6 class at my school an adult noticed that a group of children displayed an interest in ice hockey. She noted it and, with the teacher, incorporated it into some design and technology planning – children created team uniforms and a new stadium design.

Involve children in planning: The planning circle

A great way to incorporate engagement and children's interests into a theme is to get the children to plan for you! It saves you time and also makes them feel like they have invested in their learning. Get the children in a circle and present the topic. Imagine that the topic for the half term is space. Start by asking your class: what do they want to know about space and what do they already know? Depending on the age group, you could stay in the circle and lead this as a whole-class activity or, if the children are older, ask them to make groups and create a mind map. They can write the questions they want answered on a planning sheet. If leading a planning circle with younger children, get them to talk to each other or look at some books related to the topic before you ask them questions and then collate them together on one big planning sheet. Here are some examples of questions produced in a planning circle that was done with a Year 5 class in my school:

- How long does it take to get to the moon?
- What is the Earth made of?
- Is there life on Mars?
- What does an astronaut wear?
- How can we communicate with astronauts in space?
- What is NASA?
- Did a dog go into space?
- Has anyone stepped on Jupiter?
- What are the rings of Saturn made of?
- How many stars are there in our galaxy?

Next, the teacher created a learning board with these questions at the centre. They were the starting point for the lessons that followed. Here are some examples:

- **History:** first man on the moon, the first dog in space, the establishment of NASA
- **Design and technology:** astronaut suit designs, models of planets
- **Literacy:** letters to NASA, stories about space journeys, newspaper report of the dog's journey into space, alien descriptions and stories about alien invasions
- **Science:** testing of materials for astronaut suits, making an electrical circuit to light a star
- **Maths:** journey times, distances.

There are lots of possibilities here, but the important thing is that the children see that their ideas have been valued. As your planning display develops, you can add examples of learning from the children and answers to the questions they have asked. I have seen learners go home and research questions themselves and this has been added to the wall. This approach nurtures curiosity and lets the children explore – these are crucial skills to develop a growth mindset.

Encourage deep thinking: The big questions

Children need opportunities to think deeply and respond. It builds their ability to explore ideas and to use what they already know to comment on things. In your school, create a board that has a 'big question' on it. You could change the question weekly or every half term. Provide sticky notes or equivalent for the children to respond and post their thoughts. Some examples of 'big questions' could be:

- If you were king or queen for the day, what would you do?
- How would you save the rainforests?

- Should animals be tested on so make up is safe to use?
- What would you like to study at university?
- Imagine you were a newspaper editor today, what would your headline be?
- Should sugar be banned and why?

There are hundreds of examples of 'big questions', but just getting the children to think and respond is the key. They will use what they already know to make comments that relate to their own experiences. As it is a central display they will also be able to read other children's responses, which gives them an opportunity to see other points of view. Every now and then, it is a good idea to model the big question – you could bring it to assembly and ask children to respond there.

Allow them to present their ideas: Displays

Encourage the children to take an active role in displays. Give the children an opportunity to suggest ideas on what would be good on a display and what they could create. Where possible, let the learners lead on displays and give them opportunities to build up the display over a period of time. Allow these displays to show the children's individualism and their differing approaches. There are lots of ways you can get children involved with displays, but here are some examples from my own experience:

- In Year 1 we looked at the book *Aliens Love Underpants* by Claire Freedman and Ben Cort and asked the children what learning we could create. They then offered suggestions on what could be displayed and how we could show our learning. (We even let them use the sticky tack!) In keeping with CoEL, this was a good way for children to be involved in planning an outcome and achieving what they set out to do.

An example of planning ideas for a display

- In Reception we gave children a blue tarpaulin to work on. Then, we asked the children what would be under the sea. This provided so many opportunities for learning. Groups of children researched books to find animals. Children used different materials to make different animals. A group of children were particularly interested in mermaids, so we provided the materials to make play dough ones and took photos. The children watched the display build up over two weeks and were involved in the planning throughout.

Child-led displays – give children the power to create displays

Working walls – are they really 'working'?

A working wall (WW) is an interactive display that links to the learning taking place in the classroom in the moment. It should be changed and updated regularly. As well as showcasing successful learning, it should also include examples of common mistakes that have been made in the classroom. If used properly they can support the learners to work independently and to seek out answers when they are stuck. They are usually used for English and maths, but science and topic WWs also encourage interactive learning.

The key to a WW is understanding its purpose. Here are the key things to remember:

- It is not a normal display
- It is a continual reference for learning for the children

- It contains examples of the children's work
- It has key principals of learning the children can use independently
- It is changed regularly and links to the learning taking place in the lessons.

The list of ideas for a WW is endless, but it is important that it links to the learning taking place in the lessons that week or term and that the adults in the classroom model how to use it to aid learning. WWs are most successful when you begin to see children referring to them during a lesson for guidance or ideas. It is also important that the children contribute to the walls, you can use mini activities for this and then stick them on the wall as a reminder. Below are some ideas:

- **Literacy:** Drafts of work, exemplar writing examples, key words, sentences that have been built up and improved, interesting vocabulary on sticky notes, pictures to inspire, improved descriptions.
- **Maths:** Modelled examples, reminders of symbols, visuals of concepts (e.g. fraction wall), photos of practical methods you may have completed as a class.

Here are some ideas that can help you push your WW even further:

- **Add 'Prove it' to your WW as a challenge for children**. Add a statement related to the topic and ask the children to prove it by showing how it is solved. They can add their answers to the WW.
- **Add 'The answer is…' statements.** For example, on your maths WW you could write, 'The answer is 54'. See how many questions the children can come up with that answer 54. On the literacy WW you could write, 'The answer is spooky house' and ask the children to come up with a question to complete it – the more inventive the better!
- **Create a 'Mistake Mountain'.** The idea of this concept is to show how mistakes help us 'climb' up the mountain of learning. It is an opportunity to display mistakes in the children's learning and then subsequently show how they have been addressed by the learner. The main purpose is to show how mistakes help learning and develop understanding and they should be talked about as a learning tool. By highlighting them, they stop becoming something to be worried about and something to be celebrated. Regularly add a piece of work to the wall with some mistakes – this could be done by your TA or another adult. Place this on the mistake mountain and ask the children to correct the mistakes or spot them. Be as creative as you like with this display (any mountain will do)!
- **Challenge learners to 'Make it better'.** A good addition to a literacy WW is a passage with no punctuation. Ask the children to rewrite the passage using correct punctuation – display their examples to show how they have improved it.

Learning walls

It is key that children can see the outcomes of their learning. A learning wall for any age group is an excellent way to do this. Show the children visually how learning develops and unfolds. For

Display visual learning journeys

example, use your learning wall to begin a topic by displaying the learners' questions and then as you travel through the topic and learn more, add them visually to the wall – this could be pieces of the learners' work, photographs or items from home. The aim is to show them that learning is a process rather than an instant result. A learning wall should showcase the children's journey. You could allocate individual sections for each child and give them the opportunity to display what they have learnt or any questions they still have. Encourage them to replace or add to their section of the wall as they learn. They could replace their question with the answer if they have found it. The learning wall is a brilliant reference to show progress because children can compare learning and look at the improvements. This opens up discussion about why it is better. The learning wall is an ongoing visual record of progress. The whole wall can be put into a class book at the end of each term, which is a great reference for progress and curriculum coverage. This is an instant display of progress not only for the children but also for other visitors to the school.

Summary

When thinking about introducing a growth mindset culture in your setting, reflecting on the learning attitudes across the whole school and comparing them to the Early Years CoEL and Development Matters is a good place to begin. Hopefully, the practical suggestions in this chapter have provided you with a starting point. They will help you to make sure children feel unique and make learning personalised – this, in turn, creates an enabling environment. The children should feel part of the learning process in order for them to understand how they can change their own learning journey with the right mindset. Chapter 2 is intended to help children feel empowered in their own learning decisions and to feel excited about challenge rather than defeated by failure.

To do list

- Observe your classes – are the CoEL still being promoted throughout the school?
- Take a learning walk and review how child-led your school is.
- Create ways that children can explore their own individuality and what makes them special.
- Encourage all adults to contribute to planning based on children's interests.
- Think about how planning involves the children – introduce planning circles.
- Host staff workshops on effective WWs. Select someone who is using them effectively and get them to mentor others.
- Think about making displays more interactive so that the children feel a part of them.

Chapter 2

Reach for the Stars – differentiation with a difference

Picture this scene. A teacher hands out a selection of worksheets to the class. Different groups of children receive different worksheets. The result is that one group of children, let's call them the green group, are given a clear message they are the brightest in the class. In contrast, another group, let's call them the red group, feel demotivated before they have even started working because they realise they have been given a 'differentiated' worksheet. I'll always remember Year 4 pupil who once said to me, 'I always knew I was bad at maths because I got a worksheet from the small pile'.

Of course, it is important to provide differentiation because not all children have the same abilities. Learning should be personalised to a child's ability, with a level of challenge built in. However, if differentiation is too apparent in the classroom, the message it promotes can actually limit learning. Children understand why they are sat at the front and why they have been given a different worksheet from everyone else. The message they get is clear: 'you can't do it'. Worksheets limit learning and box children up because they create a culture where challenge is seen as only being for other people. It is not just the lower ability pupils who are affected: this also limits higher ability children because it creates a pressure to be perfect, meaning they feel that if they can't complete the 'top work' they have failed. Neither of these scenarios promotes a growth mindset or encourages healthy learning behaviours for life. So, how do we give children tasks that they can achieve without limiting them? How can we ensure all children feel challenged?

A growth mindset classroom acknowledges that sometimes tasks are hard. There are strategies put in place that mean that the child feels that challenge is positive and knows that asking for help or independently finding ways to solve the task are equally encouraged.

Reach for the Stars

When a teacher delivers a lesson, the task following the input is usually decided on behalf of the children and allocated according to ability. This approach creates learners that don't make learning decisions for themselves and aren't independently creating challenge or developing the desire to push themselves. In short: it's limiting. In the Reach for the Stars (RFTS) programme the children get to choose their task, which means that they choose their own level of challenge and make independent choices about what task they believe they can tackle. Be careful of differentiated worksheets, choice isn't just picking one of these. The choice could lie in how they decide to tackle a task or present their work. Be creative with how children can manage their own ability level and challenge themselves. There are many interesting ways this can be done and there are some suggestions below. I have seen whiteboards on working walls with different activities on, different tasks on different tables to choose from, a challenge wall with three sets of tasks.

The following case studies are examples of RFTS in action. They are intended to give you some inspiration for how you can incorporate differentiation into your lesson without labelling children according to their ability.

Case Study 1

A Year 5 teacher delivered a literacy lesson on the text the class have been reading – *Sherlock Holmes* by Sir Arthur Conan Doyle. The learning objective was to deduce information about a character in the book. The teacher provided three differentiated activities: Stargazer, Constellation and Shooting Stars (each providing a different challenge). Here's the clever bit – the children did not know the ability level of each activity, all they had were the names. Moreover, these get changed regularly, which meant that no pattern of ability group was formed. The teacher also provided a further activity, Astronomer, which was a mastery activity that learners could move on to once they have finished the main activity.

Children were given one minute to discuss which activity they would choose, which meant that they felt empowered to achieve in their own way. They gave themselves a challenge based on their own ability and which task they felt that they most wanted to tackle. And, because they didn't know the levels of differentiation, they didn't feel they had been labelled before they had even started.

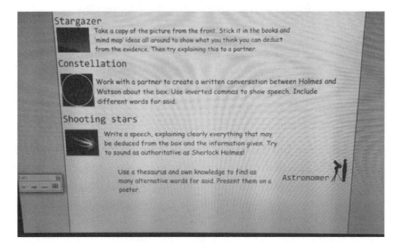

An example of Reach for the Stars options

Case Study 2

A Year 1 class were investigating changes in materials. The teacher prepared frozen balloon eggs wrapped in newspaper and they spent time exploring these, with great excitement! The teacher asked the children to write words on sticky notes to describe what they could feel throughout the exploration. They were also asked questions throughout the activity including, how has the teacher put the ice into the balloons? The pupils were then given a choice of RFTS activities:

- Stargazer: Write a sentence on a whiteboard explaining how the ice got into the balloons.

- Constellation: Join a carpet discussion to write together how the ice got into the balloons.

- Shooting star: Draw and write a comic strip that explains how the ice got into the balloons.

- Astronomer: Create a word bank of your observations.

Engaging different learners

The children were given one minute to choose their activity. The Constellation carpet discussion was led by the LSA in the classroom. When I observed this lesson, it struck me that I had already mentally made a prediction, based on my prior knowledge of the children, about which children would choose which activity. But, I was wrong and I'm happy I was! I saw boys who I considered lower ability writers who could not wait to grab their whiteboard. There was a real shift in the learning culture in the classroom. The Constellation group were engaging in a rich discussion, using scientific language and higher thinking skills. In the Shooting Star group children were transferring and applying their knowledge to create a comic strip.

Concern busting

RFTS is a different way of providing differentiation in your classroom and, at first, you might have some doubts about how effective it can be. But, give it a go and you will see for yourself the results in can produce! In my experience I have encountered many staff and parents who are sceptical about the effectiveness of RFTS before they have seen it in action. Here, I have outlined some of the most frequent concerns I have heard and my explanation. I hope that this might allay any fears that you might have and show you how effective this framework can be.

'I bet all the pupils choose the easy task'

This is a comment I have faced many times. However, it's our pessimism about children that leads to this assumption. As has been established through learner interviews and rigorous monitoring, children want to learn, they want to progress, and they want to challenge themselves. Introducing this system creates a culture where 'hard' is embraced, challenge is applauded, and children make independent choices. The majority of children will choose their own level and want to succeed in their choice. The teacher and LSA will quickly identify the odd pupil who chooses an activity that is not suited to them. This highlights their learning behaviours, which is a good thing. Why is a child choosing to undersell themselves? Why are they afraid of failure? What can we do to support this?

'What if they make a mistake? Or, even worse, fail?'

This is another comment I've heard frequently. In a growth mindset culture, the words 'mistake' and 'fail' are seen as positive learning steps. It is good for a child to know what it is like to make a mistake – what could they do next time to avoid it? In a fixed mindset culture, children don't make mistakes because the worksheet or task is modelled in such a way that they never will. But, ultimately, this means they never understand how to learn from them. When a child makes a mistake or feels they haven't achieved, it is a golden opportunity to explore what went wrong. How could you improve the learning? What could you have done?

How do I introduce RFTS?

When you first introduce the RFTS approach in your classroom, start with one subject at a time. So, for example, start by only using it in maths. This gives the children a chance to understand the new approach and also gives the teachers and staff a bit of thinking time! It is a completely new approach and it may need some tweaking so that it is appropriate for the children in your class. Once established in one subject, roll it out to other subjects in the timetable. The children will become very used to the new approach after a short period of time.

Work as a teaching team

When you first introduce RFTS, it is a good idea to decide on what tasks to offer as a team. Share learning objectives for a lesson and decide on the Stargazer, Constellation, Shooting Stars and Astronomer activities. If you use a scheme for maths, the activities are already written but, remember, the key is to let the children choose. It is important that they do not know the level of each activity and that they only have one minute of thinking time to choose their activity. Supporting independence is the key. (How to set up your classroom and resources to support their independent choices is explored in more detail in Chapter 4.)

Astronomer activities

The Astronomer activity is an activity for children to explore and consolidate the learning. This could be an application task and is for children to work towards once they have finished their chosen RFTS activity. You could display it on the working wall or in the classroom. Here are some examples of astronomer tasks:

The answer is...

In this activity you provide the answer and children have to figure out the question that fulfils this answer. For example, stick 25 sticky notes in a square on the board and above it write, 'The answer is 25cm'. This is a great way for children to explore the many different questions and solutions and using trial and error helps them to understand that sometimes there is more than one answer. It is always good to challenge the children to think of a complicated question and they will rise to this challenge. Here are some more ideas: 'The answer is... red, 1500, ¾ of a field'.

Practise power

When I look at books from children in the first few year groups, I often see very sophisticated marking but find that mistakes concerning basic skills have been ignored. The Practise Power (PP) method shows children that sometimes you only get results from practising. In your school assign a highlighter colour to be used for PP across the whole school – let's say it is blue. In learners' books highlight basic skills errors (e.g. the misformed b or the seven that is back to front). Children are told that when they see the PP highlight it means they need to practise the correct version underneath their learning ten times. Allocate PP time or ask children to look for highlighted PP in other small windows of time in the day. Children need to hear the message that things improve when you practise them a lot.

Are you sure you understand? Show it... Grow it!

Provide a box containing different question starters and ask the children to select a starter and complete it in relation to the learning of the day. This helps them to consolidate and master learning.

Some examples of question starters are:

- Can you draw…
- Teach your friend…
- How accurate is…
- Can you show… another way?
- Find out how…
- Can you investigate…

Prove it or lose it

Ask the children to prove the answers to problems using a written method. This works well in maths if you give them a completed calculation, e.g. '345 × 3 = 1,035 – prove it'. You can make these statements word statements as well, e.g. 'Andrew says his garden is bigger than John's – prove it'. Here you can include pictures of two different shapes that challenge the learners' view on perimeter. There are endless ways to ask the children to explore the process they went through to get to a certain result and, as we know, learners with a growth mindset aren't just interested in the outcome but the process too. You can link 'prove it' to English tasks too, e.g. 'Oliver Twist is a lovely boy – prove it'. It is well worth working as a team to create 'prove its' – a staff meeting could generate a term's worth for everyone!

Peer learning

Peer learning is low cost and high impact when it comes to progress. In the classroom it can be used as an Astronomer task to help the child consolidate their own learning. For example, ask them to create a leaflet explaining a topic to a peer. The process of creating the leaflet helps embed the learning. It also means they can share their learning with other children in other classes if time permits.

How can you make sure children understand their learning process?

If children can see their learning develop, they will start to make links to their effort. They will know how hard they have worked in a particular area and will be able to see how this impacts their results.

Achievement line

An easy way to help children to see their learning is through the use of an achievement line. An achievement line is simply a scale from one to ten. You can print these off and get children to stick them in their books to save time. At the very beginning of the lesson, after you have explained what they will be learning, ask them to score on their line how confident they are of their understanding of that topic or concept. For example, in a lesson is about adverbs, ask children to score how confident they are that they know what one is, know how to use one, know a variety of adverbs and can change an adjective to an adverb. At the end of the lesson ask them to mark a second score on the line to show how confident they feel now. Most will give themselves a higher score than they gave themselves at the beginning of the lesson. It doesn't have to happen in every lesson but it is a useful task to do occasionally to help children to make the link between effort and learning results.

To mix things up, you could have one huge achievement line in the classroom and laminated images of the children's faces or names. At the beginning of the lesson ask them to put their name or face on the number they feel signals where they are and then move it to show where they think they are when they leave the classroom.

Grow boxes

Give the children a 5cm x 5cm box. Show them the learning for the lesson and ask them to write everything they know about it in the box in one colour. For example, if the lesson is about the human heart, children can draw a picture of a heart or write words that show what they know about what the heart does and why it's important. Explain that by the end of the lesson their learning will have grown, so they need to leave room in their box to write more words. At the end of the lesson ask the children to add what they have learnt in a different colour in their grow box. Most children will be very happy with the result because they will see clearly that in an hour they have learnt many things.

Austin's butterfly

Austin's Butterfly is a famous learning video and is easily accessible online. The idea originated in America and it is all about showing how feedback helps us to develop and get better. The practitioner in the video starts by drawing a butterfly and asks the children to give feedback on how to make it better. The practitioner encourages the feedback to be specific, e.g. curve the wings. After they have received the feedback, the practitioner re-draws the butterfly. After

Creating their own 'Austin's butterfly'

several attempts and rounds of feedback, it looks much better! This video demonstrates the power of targeted feedback and how it can improve learning. Using this as a starting point with children can help to teach them how to give and receive quality feedback – the principles can then be applied to many different activities.

You can find it on YouTube here: www.youtube.com/watch?v=dOSiU42P8Gc.

This activity is all about getting children to understand how improvement takes time and requires listening to feedback. This feedback can be used to produce a better outcome. When leading my own Austin's Butterfly in my school we asked children to draw an animal. Then, we shared their drawings with the rest of the class, who were asked to give feedback about what worked well and how they could make their drawing better. Next, they drew the same picture again, taking on board the feedback they had received. We then compared the two drawings and discussed the progress.

It is an excellent way to show children how feedback can make a positive contribution on their outcome and helps them to explore their process. You can link it to your topic or area of learning and make it a discrete lesson. I have also seen it done successfully when drawing feathers to support learning about the book *Skellig* by David Almond. Having these displayed in the classroom is a brilliant reference point for teachers because it proves the point that our first attempt can always be improved; the skills in this activity can be applied across the curriculum.

Draft wall

Once you have embedded the process of learning through your own Austin's Butterfly activities you can transfer this work to a draft wall. This is an ongoing working wall that shows how feedback can change learning. Start with a piece of the children's learning and show that it has been improved with feedback. You can use speech bubbles to show the feedback given. There are two clear objectives to this process. Firstly, the children learn that acting upon quality feedback improves learning and, secondly, children understand how to give and receive quality feedback. Use this as a visual tool to show how learning changes with feedback. You can apply it to art, design and history projects and all areas of the primary curriculum.

On your draft wall display clearly the 'expected' and 'exceeding' statements. Underneath these, display writing examples from your class. As you go through the week or learning period, take a moment to analyse the work on the draft wall and talk to children about the positives and where it could be improved. Ask the class to help improve it and then display the improved version. The draft wall will continually change according to feedback from adults and children. As a headteacher, I sometimes pop into classrooms and spend five minutes contributing to the wall – this reinforces that feedback comes from many sources. It creates a culture where children understand that the first time is not the only time – we can change, accept feedback and make it even better. Help them to understand the process by making this a firm part of the classroom culture.

Summary

Reach for the Stars is a method that helps children to feel that they have choice in their learning outcomes and can challenge themselves. It creates an environment where children are not limited before they even start. By modelling growth, the importance of feedback and how it takes many attempts to improve something, you show children of all abilities that they can use these skills to help them to achieve their own personal learning goals. Chapter 3 discusses and includes ideas on how to build the confidence of children of all abilities and to give them the skills to develop their own healthy learning attitude for life.

To do list

- Introduce choice for children to include challenge for all abilities.
- Work as a teaching team to devise ideas for these choices – steer away from worksheets and look at more open-ended tasks.
- Use Astronomer activities to help children consolidate, apply knowledge and examine their processes to get to answers.
- Consider how your school helps children explore their process of learning.
- Embed how we can improve our learning with feedback within the classroom environment.

Chapter 3

'I sit with the thick kids who are just like me'

As part of my research for this book, I observed many different classes and I noticed that many of them were set up in a stereotypical way. Certain groups of children were always sat together – children who were considered lower ability were all positioned at the front or, at the very least, near the front. There is lots of research that shows that using ability groups does not actually help children to progress; instead, there is evidence to suggest that it limits them. Although there is still some debate on this topic, I can say for certain that sitting children in ability groups does not support the message of a growth mindset.

Considering the pressure that is placed on teachers to ensure that children reach certain targets, it is understandable that streaming might seem an obvious solution. Streaming is commonplace in secondary schools, but now it is becoming more and more prevalent in primary schools too. (I have visited schools where phonics is streamed in Year 1!) However, I propose that if a school wants to embed a growth mindset, streaming does not work. When children are streamed, they know their groups – we may think they don't, but they do. It sends a message that you are only as good as the group you are in. This affects self-esteem. Therefore, streaming doesn't support the message that effort, resilience and mistakes equal growth in learning. In my opinion, the only way to ensure all children are given open-ended opportunities is to avoid streaming and find other ways to facilitate challenge. The learning environment should create learners with healthy opinions of their own abilities.

The classroom set-up

This starts with the classroom set-up. I have observed many lessons where the additional adults in the classroom always sit with the lower ability group. Meanwhile, children considered higher ability are usually positioned at the back of the classroom and are pretty much left to their own devices. In my observations, I also found that this seating arrangement did not necessarily change for different subjects. This means that some children do not get the opportunity to work with different learning partners and are not exposed to different learning styles or expectations, despite the fact that their ability might differ in each subject. I asked some of the teachers if they could explain more about the reasoning behind their seating plan and their deployment of additional adults. Here are some of the responses I received:

- They need the most support, so it's easier to have them all together.
- Differentiation is easier because they all have the same work.
- The back tables don't need an adult as much.
- Their behaviour needs managing, so it is easier if they are all sat together.

As a practitioner or a leader in a school, you may agree with these statements. However, if you are committed to a growth mindset culture, you will realise that these messages do not promote it. Think about what this kind of seating plan is communicating to the children. It means that you are not stretching their expectations of themselves – you are putting them into boxes that have limits. To have a true growth mindset culture you should be exploring independent learning for all the children. How can they reach their own potential based on their decisions? Let me quickly recap on the characteristics of a growth mindset. Someone with a growth mindset:

- is a challenge seeker;
- does not ignore talents and believes that talents can be grown;
- believes that learning can improve over time;
- is eager to explore new topics and subjects.

When we think about these characteristics it is clear that the way learners feel about themselves in the classroom is fundamental to growth. So, ask yourself: is the classroom set-up and environment promoting self-worth, self-reflection and high self-esteem? Do they feel they are challenging themselves? Are they building daily on talent and learning? Do they have high expectations of themselves?

Hot desking: How to make it work

There are many different ways you can set up your classroom to facilitate a growth mindset. One particularly effective way is through hot desking. Hot desking in the classroom is the same as it is in an office environment. It is giving learners an opportunity to regularly sit somewhere different, depending on the task they are completing. This prevents ability groups from forming and gives children the opportunity to support each other's learning. To begin with, hot desking can take some time to get used to but, once established, it is really effective. However, don't be afraid to move children if they are not working effectively.

Here are some ideas on how to use hot desking in the classroom. All of these ideas can be used throughout the week. Practitioners can decide which lessons they will work best in, but all of them give learners opportunities to work with many different learners and to experience peer learning.

- Once the learning objective for the lesson has been revealed, give children the Reach for the Stars options (see Chapter 2). After they have chosen their task, allow them to sit with children who are completing the same task.

- Assign every child a 'learning buddy'. It is important that these are mixed ability. Keep learners in the same pairs for at least a term so they can build up a rapport. Throughout the week, plan lessons where children work with their learning buddy, even if this is just to sit together and work independently and afterwards give them the opportunity to discuss their learning. Once the system is in place, you can just call out, 'learning buddies' and the children will know where to go.

- Assign a child to be the 'teacher of the table'. It is this child's responsibility to take notes for the table during the whole-class teaching – you could even give them an iPad® or tablet to film it. When the children begin the consolidation of the skills they have just been taught, this learner is responsible for answering questions and helping the group. For younger children you can even buy some cheap glasses for them to wear – it makes it feel very important! Change the 'teacher of the table' regularly to give all children the opportunity to take on the role.

Building resilience

We want children to be resilient, determined and have the ability to be motivated without the constant need for reward. To do this we have to teach children how to have effective learning behaviours for life. When I began researching the children in my school's mindset I had some disturbing discussions with children about how they saw teaching and learning. Below are some statements that children gave me when I asked them general questions about how they felt about their learning, where they sat in the classroom and what they achieved in their school day.

- 'I know I'm thick, I always have a sheet from the small pile.' (Year 5 pupil)
- 'I have to sit at the front in the bottom group.' (Year 4 pupil)
- 'My teacher gives me the work I can do – the harder stuff is for the clever ones.' (Year 2 pupil)

I find it hard to believe that we are still using the terms higher, middle and lower ability in classrooms. These terms set children their limits before they have even begun. Consider a child who has been treated as lower ability since Year 1. What learning behaviours does that child have by Year 6? Have they had six years of sitting at the front? Have they had six years of working in a 'special group'? Have they had six years of receiving the small pile of worksheets because that is what they can do? Equally, the message for the higher ability children is, 'You are clever and always sit at the back'. This message is equally damaging as when they do experience a difficult challenge, they struggle to overcome it and so ultimately give up.

So, how do we find the balance between providing work that is suitable for each ability without putting children into boxes that mean they never feel challenge or independence? You can use Reach for the Stars (see Chapter 2) and the other similar methods to differentiate work, but you also need to focus on building children's self-esteem. Provide them with their own toolbox of learning strategies and resilience, so they know that hard things are a good thing.

Use books as a platform for explaining that mistakes are good

Using stories is a great way to introduce the idea that mistakes are good, particularly with younger children. This can be a hard concept for some children to accept. This depends on the messages they have received in their external life. A continual flow of mindless affirmations can be damaging because it promotes the idea that mistakes are bad.

The book, *The Girl Who Never Made Mistakes,* written by Mark Pett and Gary Rubinstein is a good way to introduce children to the idea that being perfect doesn't allow for learning. You can use it in assemblies or read it at story time in your classroom. Ask the children when they have made a mistake: how did it feel? What could they learn from it?

Here is a list of other books that are useful for building the culture of resilience:

- *The Day the Crayons Quit* by Drew Daywalt and Oliver Jeffers
- *The Lion Inside* by Rachel Bright and Jim Field
- *Giraffes Can't Dance* by Giles Andres and Guy Parker-Rees
- *Ish* by Peter H. Reynolds

Story sacks

As with all books, I recommend you read them as a whole class, but you can also give children an opportunity to experience them on a more personal level. Display them in your school entrance and allow parents and children to borrow them for the night and bring them back with a review of what they learnt.

Create 'story sacks' to accompany books. A 'story sack' is a bag containing a book and some props and items that are featured in the book. This brings the story alive. For example, in a story sack for *The Day the Crayons Quit* you might include: letters, envelopes, crayons, rainbow colour charts, black card for the white crayon, a selection of items mentioned in the book such as a toy elephant, a plastic apple, a fire engine, a toy crocodile and lastly a piece of white paper for the readers to use all the crayons.

'Story sacks' are something parents love to get involved with. They do not need to cost a lot of money. It is handy to have a laminated list of what is in the sack, so that you can maintain them. Children can borrow them to share with their family for a weekend. (Who doesn't love a cuddly giraffe? Or crayons they can use?) Put challenge cards in the sacks to encourage discussion and reflection. Some examples are: draw a picture that uses every colour; write a well done note to yourself for having courage; write instructions for yourself on how you can achieve something you can't do yet or teach your family what courage means. Use your social media to share the 'story sacks'. Tweet children's thoughts and ideas or upload a video review of the book. Use hashtags, for example: #ish #giraffescantdance.

(Note: when using social media, always issue consent forms and remind parents not to include names of the children when posting online.)

Mistakes

Model mistakes

Teachers should be modelling mistakes, even if this means manufacturing some. (Although in my experience I have had many mind blanks when spelling a word on a board!) Get into the habit of encouraging your teachers to embrace and highlight their own mistakes. Make it a positive culture where TAs feel they can correct teachers mistakes and vice versa – think of each other as a critical friend.

Spot the mistake

Have regular activities that allow children to correct mistakes, using dictionaries or maths resources. This helps children to understand that the mistake doesn't matter – it is how you rectify it and what you learn from it that matters. Make this part of regular teaching and include examples on your working walls.

Newsletter mistakes

Make it a weekly competition for children and adults to find the grammatical or spelling mistake in the weekly newsletter – this also helps make sure that your parents and learners are reading it! Make them hard to find and then highlight them in the next week's edition.

Get ready it's tough (GRIT)

It is important that children learn that hard work pays off. As practitioners, we often avoid this statement for fear of putting children off learning. Sometimes we try to praise every little thing that children do but this often becomes a bit false. Start telling the children the truth in a positive way. For example, 'Yes that's a good start, I like your first sentence, to make it better you should…'. The message that hard work will equate eventually to a more positive outcome in all areas of life is an important statement for children to hear regularly. Use the acronym GRIT to remind children that sometimes things are difficult, but it is important that we keep going – overcoming challenges make us stronger. Demonstrate this by creating a display of pictures or use your social media to celebrate children who have embraced tough challenges and kept going. Again, model GRIT if you can and include staff in your displays. At our school our moment of GRIT was completing a walking marathon at night – the children loved hearing about it and we involved the parents through social media.

You can extend GRIT to your classroom. Provide open-ended challenges, such as puzzles, games and brainteasers, that really need determination to get results. Having a 1000-piece puzzle in the classroom is a great motivator for a five-minute GRIT break. In my role as a headteacher I have a puzzle table in my office – I can model doing it to the children and it is a great activity to build self-esteem for children who are struggling to value their own learning moments.

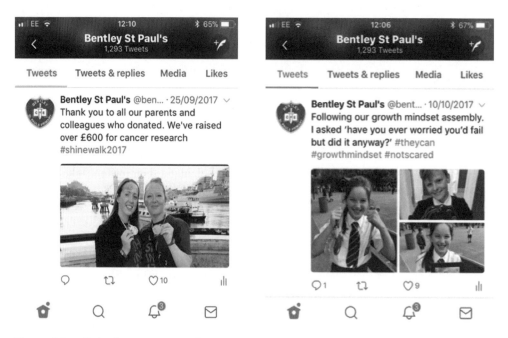

Use social media to share messages of growth mindset regularly

Reflection

In recent years the importance of mindfulness and reflection has become an increasingly prominent part. In education it can be used to help children to reflect on their own achievements, plan their goals and be able to verbalise what they need to do next or indeed what they have achieved and are proud of. It is even more important to reflect on how they achieved it.

Journaling

There is a lot of research to suggest that journaling is a particularly positive way to reflect and to help adults and children see the progress they are making in life – often we overlook the small things and journaling can help to highlight all achievements. Journaling is a powerful tool for adults and children because it gives us opportunities to be individual and to reflect on a certain topic. Provide children each with a high-quality journal and allow them to make it their own. (I am a self-confessed stationery addict and have many journals that are all hardback bound and beautiful!) Encourage children to regularly write in their journal things they have learnt or achieved in the classroom, draw pictures or even stick in pieces of work that they are proud of or have learnt from. You can easily build journaling time in to your lessons by encouraging children to take a few minutes to write in their journal throughout the week. Start by giving them some prompts.

Prompts for pages could include:

- My goals and dreams
- What I have learnt this week?
- My mistake mountain (see Chapter 2)
- When have I needed courage?
- Things I am proud of
- Books I have learnt from
- People who inspire me
- Monthly goals list
- What do I want to know by the end of year?

You can find lots of ideas on Pinterest – bullet journals are a great source of inspiration. Remember pages can be returned to over time. For example, children can add to their mistake mountain whenever they make a mistake and learn from it. Children will get into the habit of recording things that happen to them or things they are thinking about in their journal. The key is, there are no rules! Children can use pictures, felt tips, crayons, words, mindmaps, photographs – whatever they choose, allow their creativity to take over. In the past I have had children who have asked for pieces of work to be photocopied for their journal or they have brought in pictures of achievements from home they wanted to stick in. Let them go for it!

Modelling is crucial for this process, so the teacher and additional adults should also have a journal. The children love to see adults' journals and it also promotes staff wellbeing because it gives staff time to reflect on their own learning journeys. To begin with, allow 15 minutes to model a starter journal point. An example of a starter could be:

- My goals for June
- My strengths
- Things that make me happy
- This week I will…
- I dream of…

You may want to trial journaling in one class first and then you can ask the teacher who has done the trial and the students in that class to help cascade it throughout the school. You can give them the task of telling the rest of the staff and children in the school what went well and what could have gone better.

Children should be encouraged to take their journal home and complete unfinished pages or share with their families. All the children I have worked with have loved this opportunity. I have also set up a classroom at lunchtime for a journal club to enable children to have the opportunity to journal in school.

In the classroom, journals are for the individuals so you can display them but keep the contents confidential. Teach the children to respect each other's journals by explaining that they are a collection of ideas, thoughts and reflections that are individual and special to each person. Journaling improves self-esteem because it encourages children to see themselves as not comparative to others. Children answer the questions and reflect independently which means they are less concerned with giving the 'right' answer and can be more honest in their responses and explore what they think about themselves. If you asked a class of children to write down their strengths in their journals you would probably find that nearly every child had written something different. When we stop comparing ourselves we can give ourselves the space to see our own strengths. If we teach children early in life to examine themselves and their strengths, it will improve their self-esteem later in life.

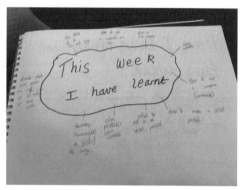

Examples of journal prompts and questions for metacognition

Effective intervention: Additional adults

Having additional adults in the classroom is an amazing support for teachers. Most are very committed individuals who want the best for the children. However, some teachers have commented that additional adults can be prone to spoon-feeding children answers. Although this is done with the best intentions, it does not encourage resilience or GRIT. In Chapter 7 I will look at effective language and feedback in more detail but, in the meantime, what can these adults be doing to really support a growth mindset culture? Here are some tips to help you get the best out of the additional adults in your classroom:

- Ensure all adults understand the importance of growth mindset – adapt the parent workshop in Chapter 8 for an initial training session with additional adults.

- Acknowledge everyone's contribution to the school and value your team's effort, including those adults. This models that we are all learning and contributing.

- Have a station where the additional adults can be based. They can then focus on a smaller group of children or work with individuals one-on-one. This also gives the children the opportunity to move, rather than always sitting in the same place.

- Train all staff in metacognition. Metacognition is where children are explicitly taught about how they learn and are encouraged to think about this process when learning new knowledge. This means that the skills needed to learn effectively are being used and can be developed for all future learning.

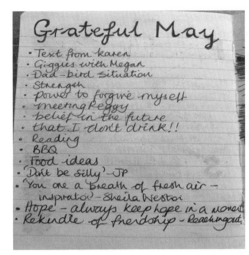 

Adult journaling – great for wellbeing and modelling to groups

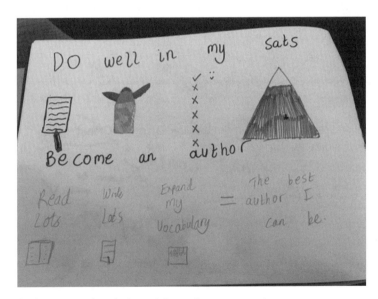

Setting personal goals through journaling

- Encourage them to model behaviour and expectations along with the teacher. They too can model mistakes, have their own journal and of course GRIT!

- Make an element of your growth mindset culture part of their performance management: how are they supporting it?

- Have a team display in the staffroom of good examples of how children have been supported as individuals and allowed to grow.

- Make individual children's targets clear, so all adults can make small steps to help them make progress. Learning passports are a brilliant example of this.

Summary

In this chapter we have explored the culture of the classroom. In today's world we need to think more explicitly about giving learners the tools to reflect on their own skills in order to learn. A classroom that encourages learners to be put into boxes means they never really explore their own potential, they never take risks or plan goals of their own.

In a growth mindset culture, reflection on an individual's achievements and their learning journey is fundamental to ensure they are all reaching their individual potential. This focuses on the individual's own responsibility to achieve and what they need to do to fulfil goals. Children who have a growth mindset understand they are the factor that can change their learning outcomes. By giving them the tools to do this, they will increasingly take more responsibility for their outcomes as they get older. The next chapter looks at independence and how important it is to develop independent learning in our young people.

To do list

- Review seating plans in the classrooms and ability groups. Are they having impact? Are they reflecting a growth mindset culture?

- Model and celebrate mistakes in classrooms.

- Create a mini library of books that carry the message of resilience for children and families to borrow and engage with.

- Ensure all adults have received growth mindset training and they recognise the importance of it to the school culture.

- Consider how children reflect on their achievements and how they plan for the future with goals and dreams.

- Consider how journaling could work in your school.

- Model everything and, as a leader, ensure that your team is modelling. Are they resilient, brave and do they show GRIT? If so, value their contribution to your culture.

Chapter 4
Independent learning – why should I do it myself?

There is a lot of pressure put on teachers to produce outcomes – they are expected to have evidence that shows that children understand and have progressed. Unfortunately, this can result in spoon-fed education. I've often observed this in classrooms I have visited. It always leaves me wondering – what can the children do on their own? This is a particularly relevant question to consider when implementing a growth mindset culture that believes we are continually learning and can grow and can overcome barriers. What is the impact of a spoon-fed culture on children as they get older? As children move through education there is more and more emphasis on independent and self-motivated learning and revision. Certainly, when preparing for GCSEs at secondary school it becomes clear that self-motivation is the key skill in effective revision. However, many teenagers struggle with independent learning – we have to ask ourselves whether this is because these skills were not introduced early enough in their educational career? It is key to instil independent learning skills into primary-aged children as early as possible. This chapter encourages you to examine what opportunities you are offering in your classrooms to get children to think and learn for themselves and suggests some practical ways that you can further support and promote independent learning. First things first, how can you assess if children in your setting are independent learners?

What does an independent learner look like?

Some of the characteristics we would expect from an independent learner are:

- They ask questions and want to solve problems.
- They are confident and can make choices.
- They have a positive can-do attitude and are self-motivated.
- They have high self-esteem and a good self-image.
- They set their own goals, which they want to understand and achieve.
- They use teachers and other adults to help them find and select their own resources.

How is independent learning being encouraged in the setting?

In order to embed an independent learning culture, school and classrooms need to embrace 'how' things are learnt and share this with their learners. Children should feel empowered by their learning and feel they have responsibility for their own success, rather than being dragged through the learning. So, let's create an environment where learners take us on a journey!

Generally, independent learners have high self-esteem and a good self-image. Learners who have higher self-esteem regard their learning as important and are more motivated to learn. It is worth assessing how these traits are addressed in your school and what opportunities there are available in your continuous provision that enable children to develop their self-image. Think about how you can make time for this on a weekly basis in your planning.

It is important that staff understand their role in building a child's self-esteem. Ask your team what their personal values are when dealing with children who need to have their self-esteem raised. Create a display in the staffroom that celebrates how individual staff have contributed to the nurturing and care of individual learners – you can include photos and quotes.

I once displayed this conversation with a Year 2 pupil during his phonics screening.

Me: You must have really practised your sounds – you know so many more now.
Child: I have been doing them a lot.
Me: Where? At home?
Child: No with Mr Joy – he's always giving me chances to practise!

It took me seconds to type this up, print it out and display it on our staffroom board. Doing small things like this shows that you recognise the adults who are taking an individual approach to learners, which promotes the culture of care and a growth mindset throughout the school. If you want to read more about how to build a culture with a focus on self-esteem, Paul Dix's book *When the Adults Change, Everything Changes* is a great starting point.

Activities to promote self-worth

Affirmations

Make a book of cards with positive affirmations on and place it somewhere in your classroom where it is accessible to children. Affirmations could include:

- I am interesting because…
- I am happy because…
- I am positive because…

Set aside time in the week where one child picks an affirmation and places it on a whiteboard or blank piece of paper. Let the children add to it during the day as they leave the classroom or during another transition time. Reflect on the affirmations at the end of the day and ask children, what makes us feel this way?

A similar technique is to have a large tin in the classroom with slips of paper next to it that have 'I can' written on. At different points during the school week, ask children to fill in and then place 'I can' statements in the tin. These are fantastic to look back on to show children's progress and they also make a great display or newsletter feature.

Create 'Proud Clouds'

Provide children with clouds or speech bubbles to take home. Ask them to comment on something they are proud of. You can create a proud cloud postbox in the pupil entrance for them to post their responses. Display these in your classroom – they will generate some great discussions. A great way to engage parents, grandparents and carers is by asking them if they want to share anything they are proud of too. Put your cloud templates online so they can be downloaded and printed off. You can of course use your social media for this too: #proudcloud

Headteacher phone calls

I love calling home when it's about something positive! I make sure that the children know that I am going to phone the parents of children who are showing particular effort, perserverance and

Introduce a proud cloud display for parents and carers to engage with

enjoying challenge. As a headteacher, I cannot tell you how excited children get when I announce I want to phone home. (The ET reference doesn't work with the children, but the occasional staff member will laugh.) It also engages parents; I let the parents tell their children afterwards that I have phoned.

Treat children as individuals from the start

You should always treat children as individuals with individual characteristics and interests because this helps them to establish their independence. Here are some ways you can support this:

- **Show and tell:** Encourage children to bring in interests or achievements from home to share with the class or in the weekly assembly.

- **Have a basket with the label 'What makes me me?':** Inside collect certificates, artefacts or other things that are important to the children. You can have this displayed centrally for all children in the school to contribute to or you can have a basket in each classroom.

- **Select a 'Special person of the week':** Make sure you select a child at random and don't base your decision on behaviour.

- **Hold a 'Me conference':** As teachers, we often attend learning to discuss academic targets and goals. Why not host one for the children? It could include discussions and questions such as: what do you enjoy about school? What's your favourite hobby? What's your favourite book? The list is endless, but the point is that you get to know the children. When I held a 'Me conference' at my school I learnt that there were a number of students who were fascinated and keen to learn the game of chess. This interest snowballed into a chess group that met regularly. The students became chess teachers who wanted to share this skill.

- **Greet learners at the door with a personalised 'Hello':** Greeting children by acknowledging or asking them about something they are interested in can make a huge difference. For example, 'Morning John, how's the new bike?', 'Morning Sarah, you look like you've been busy with your home project!', 'Morning Kelly, that looks like an interesting book – what is it about?'. I realise that time is precious in schools, but this personalised greeting is so powerful – it gets learners ready for the day ahead and makes them feel they have been acknowledged as an individual.

Learning mentors

In my experience learning mentors and peer mentors are highly effective in learning progress. Mentoring raises the self-motivation of children and gives them another form of support in addition to their teacher. Here are some ways you can implement peer learning in your setting:

- **Dictionary swap:** I love dictionaries and think all children should be taught to use one as soon as possible. Buddy up older and younger children for 20 minutes and give them a list of ten misspelt words to find in the dictionary together. Nominate 'Word

Wizards' to help other children find words if they are struggling. During breaktime, ask one of your midday assistants to write five misspelt words on the playground with chalk and ask children to correct them.

- **Reading pairs:** I know lots of schools that pair up year groups during reading week. Older children love reading with younger children, so why not foster this love throughout the school on regular occasions? Pair up two classes or pair younger and older children. You can also pair children in the same year group. But, don't be tempted to group children in terms of ability because, as already discussed, this can have a negative effect on self-esteem. There are ways of pairing children up in the same class that enables them to be stretched and for some to behave as a mentor. Mark out a clear timed session – possibly a couple of times a week. For older learners who are reading with a younger child, provide a reading journal – this is a joint book that can be used for the year or term, which lists the books the pairs have read. You can also use these as a quick activity to round-off each session. For example, ask children to write down new words they have learnt or their favourite character. (Have laminated cards with these activities ready to be added to their reading journals.) Children love to look back on these, so at the end of term celebrate this by inviting parents and carers in to meet their child's reading partner and to look at their journals.

- **Feedback trio:** Create a culture where feedback from peers is a normal part of school life. There are many different ways of doing this and it doesn't always have to be recorded. It is more important that children get accustomed to hearing feedback and next steps from peers. It also supports self-esteem by creating a time for positive affirmations about learning to be given. Establish that all feedback given in the classroom should be given as a 'trio': I like or admire; I think to improve you should and can you explain why... The age of the children will determine the specific language that you should use but keep the scaffold the same.

Expectations should be high in these sessions and it should be seen as a valuable part of the school day. They do require organisation, so discuss with your team how best to implement this. Children need to feel they are in a safe, secure and non-threatening environment in order for peer learning and assessment to be really effective. The more you practise, the more you will support a growth mindset culture where mistakes and learning new things are seen as positive not negative.

Targets and progress

In order to really achieve growth mindset and independence, children need to reflect on their own thinking and be actively aware of their learning processes. To be independent learners, motivation is key – having goals and targets that you want to achieve means you as an individual take ownership for your learning. Target-setting is a hot topic in primary schools and there is no magic answer for how to get it right but the emphasis should be on the children reflecting on their personal goals and what they need to do to achieve them.

Learning quests

Children should be given small targets regularly. Targets can come in the form of marking and feedback (see Chapter 7). Here, they come in the form of learning quests. A learning quest could be a short-term target quest. For example, to add two fractions. It is a mini-task and gives children an opportunity to break down bigger targets into manageable tasks and then to be able to see their progress quickly. Make sure the learning objective for a lesson is clearly visible. Then, let the children decide for themselves what their quest will be. For example, in a lesson where the class are learning to multiply a double digit by a single digit, Jamil's learning quest is to make sure he used his columns accurately, Erin's is to move onto two double digits, Natasha wants to make sure she writes number five the right way round. Depending on your learning and teaching models, you may have success criteria you share with the children or you may have bullets points of what progress will look like to prompt them. The key is getting the children to focus on something they want to succeed in because this generates motivation and independence. You can record their learning quests in many ways: allow children to write their quests on a large whiteboard, stick sticky notes on their desks or they could create a quest page in their journals.

This is also an excellent opportunity to use additional adults to individualise learning. The adults could monitor quests and give tips to ensure children are on track to succeed in their quest. In my school I have awarded wristbands (like the ones you get a festivals) with 'I completed my quest today' printed on. You don't always need to reward quests that have been successfully completed but acknowledging that children are taking control of their own learning decisions is important.

Writing conferences

I was introduced to the idea of writing conferences by a teacher recently as a way of setting informal targets. After children had completed a piece of independent writing, she organised a five-minute conference with them to discuss their next steps. I was overwhelmed by her organisation of the classroom and how well it worked as she was able to talk to all children at the conference table. The children were really clear on what they wanted to do to improve their writing and the discussion was collaborative and encouraging.

Journal it

I have already talked about the power of journaling in reflecting on a child's individual achievement and the journey they have had. Encourage children to create their own targets in their journals. These can be short-term goals and long-term ambitions. Create page prompts for journals such as:

- What I have learnt this week
- My learning goals for April
- My learning ladder
- What I dream of learning.

(See Chapter 3 for more journaling prompts.)

Goal boards

In my school there is a goal board where children can add their current goals, both at school or outside of school, using the template, 'I am working on…'. For example, 'I am working on a LEGO® model', 'I am working on fractions', 'I am working on my hiking scout badge'. You can get creative with these boards. A great way to organise your board is by creating a target or something similar and then children can place their goals at a beginning point and then move it onto the target when they have completed it. This is also an excellent way for adults in the school to model goal-setting because they can add their goals to the board too. You can also extend this to parents by inviting them to share their goals.

Goal timeline

Showing children what work has led to the achievement of goals is key to a growth mindset. Encourage journaling of goal timelines. Adults can model this on a larger scale. For example, I created a timeline of writing this book for the children to see. I included all the mini-goals I set for myself and showed the work that went into each one. Children really enjoyed watching me tick things off. A governor also created a timeline of how he trained for a triathlon. He included photographs and training plans. When the medal arrived at the end of the timeline, the children were very excited! The teachers in our school are now working on their own goal timelines to display and show the children – some are work related, others are of a personal nature (one of our teacher's goal is to make a dress, so she is including all the wonky mistakes on her timeline).

Other ways to promote independent learning

Take three before you ask me

Encourage children to use other resources around them before they ask an adult. Take three means the children get used to thinking about other sources of information to overcome challenges. One – ask yourself again, two – ask your neighbour, 3 – look for clues in the room.

Help desks

These can be set up around your topic of the week. On your desk include items or resources that will be useful for children in learning a particular topic. For example, on a maths help desk you may have number lines or cubes. It is important that the help desk becomes a normal part of the learning environment and children get used to finding resources.

You could also add iPads® or tablets to the help desk for some lessons. You will get an initial excitement about the prospect of using them but they become a normal part of classroom practice very quickly. Ask another adult or child to film the key concept of the lesson on the iPad®. For example, if the key concept is dividing, film the teacher demonstrating. This can then be added to the help desk so that children can watch the concept back if they need to be reminded.

Homework

Homework is a controversial subject in many schools, but it is a fantastic opportunity to promote children's interests and independent thinking. Review how homework is organised in the school. Does it reward effort and independence? Does it enable the children to have to use their skills of investigation or research to complete a task?

Set homework with an effort grading system rather than attainment – one is given for low effort and five is for super effort. Set your homework question or statement before you start your topic.

Give children the opportunity to do their homework in whatever form they want – they could respond to the task by making a booklet or a model. Before you launch this system, you may want to involve parents as this is a fantastic bridge for home learning. It doesn't always have to be recorded – you could ask them to tweet videos or photographs of their homework #myhomelearning.

Summary

This chapter has focused very much on the individual and their independent learning progression. Helping children to identify their own targets and goals will raise confidence and self-esteem and, in turn, boost their desire to make these things happen. The continual promotion of growth mindset is in the classroom has to come from adults and the school culture itself. Exploring the subject through assembly is another way to embed the message – this is explored in the next chapter.

To do list

- As a teaching team, assess whether your personal values promote high self-esteem. How are we contributing to this area as a school? Do all learners have access to opportunities to improve their self-image?
- Create a board in the staffroom that celebrates adults treating learners as individuals.
- Decide on strategies in the school that celebrate individualism and walk around the school to see if this is reflected. Do you know the children?
- Could learning mentors and peer learning be used more effectively? Do the children have opportunities to learn from each other?
- How does the school promote and encourage metacognition – when do children get an opportunity to think about how they learn and reflect on their own strategies?
- Review your homework policy – does it reflect the growth mindset culture?

Chapter 5
Assemblies – a time to learn

Assemblies are a great time to really explore growth mindset with your children. It is a prime opportunity to talk about the growth mindset and it helps ensure that your learning culture is consistent throughout the school. You can approach the key messages in a fun and interesting way. When I'm leading an assembly on growth mindset I play 'Reach for the Stars' by S Club 7. (You of course can create your own theme tune!) The theme tune lets the children know as soon as they walk into my assembly that we will be exploring how we learn and develop. There is always a sense of genuine excitement in the room in these assemblies – they have learnt the lyrics to the song and have even made up actions. Make these assemblies special to your school in whatever way works for you. You might use music, but anything that makes your assembly stand out will work. You want the children to be clear that this is growth mindset time!

It is vitally important that staff stay for this assembly because the messages are just as important for them to hear as they are for the children, so make it very clear at meetings that there is to be no sloping off to laminate or mark. It gives staff an opportunity to model growth mindset themselves. It is amazing how many staff who have started off cynical, having spent time in these assemblies, are converted to the growth mindset because they can see immediately the impact that these messages have on children. So, what does a growth mindset assembly look like?

Assembly ideas

It is important that it is really clear in your first assembly what a growth mindset is, why it is important and how it relates to our learning attitude. Sometimes we avoid being explicit about what we are trying to do, but the most successful cultures are those where learning about growth mindset is known and clear. The children need to be taught what growth mindset is and how they can achieve it for themselves. You also want to make it memorable so that children remember the key messages and look forward to the next assembly.

There are lots of assembly ideas online based on perseverance, goal setting and growth mindset – have a search and adapt them to suit your audience and your setting. Some assemblies will naturally evolve from what is happening in school and visitors that have come in to talk to the children. Next are some practical ideas for assemblies that I have found to be really effective.

Jelly brain

Using a jelly brain is a great way to launch your growth mindset assembly. It's simple: make a brain out of jelly! (Moulds are available online and sometimes in cheaper shops at Halloween.) Set your jelly brain at the front of the assembly but keep it covered. Start by talking to the children about muscles. Get them standing and do some simple exercises. Locate some muscles in the body and talk about what happens when we exercise and work our muscles – the conclusion will be that they get bigger! Most children do not know that the brain is an organ that acts the same way as a muscle.

Next, reveal your jelly brain. Ask questions to stimulate a discussion. Where is this organ in our body? What is it called? Is it a muscle? Do you think our brain gets bigger when we use it? Older children will laugh immediately and should be able to talk about it but younger children might need more prompting and explanation.

Next take a small strand of wool or string. Start with a small strand and ask a child to hold it. Explain that the string acts like the neurons in our brain. As we practise a skill or do an activity, we exercise the neurons in our brain and they expand. Connect this to an example, such as learning a new language. You can verbally suggest ways that we help our neurons get bigger. For example, playing language games, learning new vocabulary, talking to a friend or asking a teacher for help. Each time a new way of practising is introduced, ask another two children to come and hold another piece of string of a different length across the last piece – eventually creating a rather large 'spider web' effect. (You will need space for this.) In the end you should have a lot of children holding strings, which are interlinked and growing!

Main message: the brain is an organ, but it behaves like a muscle – we all need to exercise it to get it fitter!

Marshmallow neurons

This is a great follow-on assembly. Start your assembly with a picture of the jelly brain from last time and maybe some pictures of the children exercising to remind them of what they learnt. Refresh their memories on how the brain is an organ but behaves like a muscle. How can you exercise your brain? Show the children a marshmallow and ask them to pretend this is a small neuron in the brain. Explain that when we first learn something new we only have a few neurons. Use an example, such as fractions. When we practise, more neurons connect. They create pathways that mean that next time we encounter a similar problem or task it is easier for us to grasp certain concepts or work out the answer because we have already used that pathway before. Demonstrate this by threading two marshmallows together using dried spaghetti. Invite children up to attach more marshmallows with dried spaghetti.

Continue the example. When we watch a video to help us learn fractions, ask our teacher to help us with fractions or answer questions about fractions we are exercising our brain. As you give each step ask children to add more marshmallow neurons. As you work through, the children will begin to understand that hard work and practice makes connections in the brain so that area of learning grows.

Ask the children to make a neuron map of a new concept they are learning. Demonstrate how to make connections and how learning new things in new ways, practising, making mistakes and being resilient helps us learn.

Main message: neurons are pathways we can create by exercising our brain.

Break an egg

For this assembly you need some eggs and a few bowls. Set up your table at the front and explain to the children that sometimes in cooking you need to separate an egg into yolk and whites. Then ask the children if they can do that. (Believe me when I tell you every child in the room will raise their hand.)

Next, invite a child to demonstrate. Remember, it is important to celebrate mistakes, so involve an adult here to take a photograph of each attempt (this makes a great addition to your mistake wall). The first attempt will inevitably end with the egg on the floor! After each attempt reflect with the children on what we can learn from this mistake and what we could do differently next time. For example, Magda showed us we need to crack the egg against the bowl first; we learnt from Billy's attempt that we need to use the shells to separate the egg and Freddie showed us a different way by using his hand (he learnt this from YouTube!). Let lots of children have a go and then explore how sometimes we think something is going to be easy and it turns out to be a lot harder.

The main message: don't give up – learn from each attempt until you get it.

An active 'egg' assembly

F.A.I.L

Set up an assault course in the hall – a bench, some cones and some mats should do it. Invite someone up to the front to look at the assault course and then blindfold them. Ask them to complete the assault course with the blindfold on. Be on hand to assist any wobbles. The learner will find it tricky to begin with and will fail. After the first attempt, demonstrate how having another check and practice can improve their skills. Show F.A.I.L and explain it means 'First Attempt in Learning'. Ask the children to think of a time they have F.A.I.Led: did they try again or did they give up? Ask them to talk to the person sitting next to them about it. Have a display with F.A.I.L somewhere in the school after the assembly and invite the children to recall their F.A.I.Ls.

Main message: we all fail sometimes – but it is just the beginning, learn from it and carry on.

The Power of Yet

There is a wonderful Sesame Street™ song called 'Power of Yet'. You can find it easily by searching online and, if you can bear it, teach it to the children. Play them the song and remind them that we all have something we haven't learnt yet. Talk about keeping these things small and explain that targets and goals keep us motivated. Ask them to tell their friend what their 'yet' is. Invite the staff to think of their 'yet' too.

Once the children have thought of something, select a few to come to the front and tell their 'yet' to the assembly. Film them saying their 'yet' – this is an excellent one to communicate to parents via your social media. Alternatively, ask them to write it on a whiteboard and take photographs. In the past I have also got them to write it down and post it in the 'yet box', this means you can refer to it again in later assemblies and then see if anyone has achieved it. Keep the box for the children to contribute to throughout the year.

Main message: you don't know everything yet, set yourself targets to learn something new.

Video time

Videos are a great resource in assemblies. Children get excited when they see a video is going to be played. There are so many growth mindset videos online to choose from. Always watch

Regularly display assembly learning for continual growth mindset messages

them before you use them to ensure they are accurate, as I have come across some that have mixed messages. One of my favourite videos to use is called *SOAR*. In this wonderful animated short-film a young girl helps a tiny boy fly home before it's too late. It illustrates the message of not giving up even when obstacles come in your way. The themes from this movie could run over a few assemblies. After watching the video, you could do the following:

- Create speech bubbles for each character at different points in the video.
- Everyone has different ideas, so what would your flying machine look like?
- Have you ever fallen behind, in a race or another activity? How did you feel?
- Design a poster encouraging perseverance.
- What have you persevered to achieve?

Main message: we all have to persevere sometimes, even when things go wrong.

Mnemonics Challenge

Mnemonics are a great way to show children how to take control of their own learning and demonstrate that sometimes you need help to remember something. Start with the colours of the rainbow and ask them some simple questions. What order are they? And what are the colours? Show them how to use a mnemonic to remember the order and the colours, e.g. Richard of York gave battle in vain. More mnemonic examples include:

- Teach them to spell 'because' using 'big elephants can always understand small elephants'.
- Challenge them to think of a mnemonic to remember the planets in the solar system, the wives of Henry VII, the spelling of necessary.

Write what you want them to learn on the board and challenge them to think up ways to remember it. Challenge them to work on this during the week and then give them a test in the next assembly. Make sure they are hard!

Main message: sometimes things are hard – how can we help ourselves to learn these things?

Change a teacher's mindset

Ask some of the teachers to bring in an item that represents something they are learning. I was learning to sew and still am, another one of our teachers was learning to play the guitar. Prep one of the teachers to be purposely negative about what they are learning and say statements such as, 'I can't do it, I am giving up, it's too hard!'

Ask the children to persuade the teacher to have a growth mindset. What kind of things could they say? What tips do they have? Create a flip chart mind map of phrases the children give you. This is a great way to recognise the differences between a fixed and a growth mindset.

As a follow-up activity, ask the children to create posters to promote a growth mindset. You can include a picture of the teacher to add to the display. 'We showed Mr Smith how to have a growth mindset' is a great header!

Main message: when learning something new having a growth mindset will help you get better.

A really hard word to spell

Supercalifragilisticexpialidocious… Begin your assembly by playing the song – this excites the children, and everyone will join in. Then ask the children if they can spell it. Invite a volunteer to have a go. They will probably try and sound it out and have a good go but they are unlikely to get it right first time.

Ask the assembly if they can suggest any ways to help learn the spelling. You can model the look, cover, check method. Ask the children to spell the word out to each other. Show it on the projector and ask the children to memorise the letter order. Hand out paper and get children to practise writing it.

Ask another volunteer to try and spell it out on the board. It will be a really good try but probably won't be correct yet. Explain this is a hard challenge but that there are strategies to learn the word. Set the children the challenge to learn to spell the word by next week using the methods you have discussed. As the children leave the assembly give them the word on a piece of paper. In the following assembly ask a volunteer to spell it on the board – you will be amazed! Invite some more volunteers to do the same and then, as a group, discuss how they learnt it. What methods did they use? What characteristics did they need?

Main message: hard challenges should be faced, they can be overcome with practice and different strategies.

Austin's Butterfly

By this point in the book you have probably seen the clip about improving your work – Austin's Butterfly (as seen in Chapter 3). Use this same concept with the children by asking them all to bring a drawing of something you have pre-agreed to the assembly. It could be anything – a feather, a bird, an elephant. Involve the teachers in this, so that they make time before the assembly for the children to create their drawing using a pre-agreed prompt picture. It is important that teachers don't give any feedback on the drawings at this stage. Display some of the drawings at the front alongside the original picture. Ask the children how we could improve the displayed versions? Encourage them to be specific when giving feedback. For example, we could make the lines darker or use curved lines. Model constructive feedback to begin the process of developing this skill. Then ask the children to look at their own pictures: what one thing could they do to improve it? Immediately after the assembly ask the teachers to give the children an amount of time to re-do their picture with their improvements. Continue this process for a few weeks and ask teachers to display the process in their classrooms so that children can see how feedback improves their learning. You can extend this to other areas, such as writing, too. It is key that children see the process of improvement regularly.

Main message: using feedback improves our learning and helps us to get better at different skills.

My goal today is...

We focus a lot on long-term goals but it is also important for everyone to be in the present. What do I want to achieve now, today, tomorrow that will help me grow? For all learners, it is important to feel we are progressing and understand why. Asking children to focus on goals is an important skill, so create opportunities for them to explore how they will achieve them.

Begin with a flip chart with a big goal written on. For example, 'I am going to climb a mountain today' or 'I am going to write a novel today'. (The key is that this goal is probably unachievable.) Ask the children if they think this is going to happen today? Of course, there will be raucous laughter. Show them a stepladder and put the big goal at the top – you can do this using mini-whiteboards with the goal written on it.

Next, ask the children: what steps do I need to take to get to the bigger goal? What could I do today? The children will soon begin to give answers like: write down your novel idea, make notes about characters, write a chapter or go for a walk, plan a healthy diet, create a training plan. Write these on card and stand them up on the steps in between. Take a photo of this for the teachers to have in their classrooms, as it is a brilliant reminder for children about target setting.

Ask the children what their big goal is? What do they need to do today to achieve it? Ask them to write it on a sticky note and stick it up on their way out.

Main message: plan your goals and plan how you are going to achieve them daily.

Books to use in assemblies

There are some fantastic books that can be shared in assemblies to promote a growth mindset. I like to put them in a basket and make them available for children to read during the school day as well. My favourite books to use are:

- *Giraffes Can't Dance* by Giles Andreae and Guy Parker-Rees
- *You Can Do It, Bert!* by Ole Könnecke
- *The Lion Inside* by Rachel Bright and Jim Field.

Summary

Assemblies are a powerful way to get everyone together and spread the word about growth mindset, so make them regular and engaging. Children will begin to look forward to their weekly dose of growth mindset. Once you have planted the seeds of your message, these themes can continue in the school environment through displays. The next chapter looks at how to make displays more than wallpaper and create an interactive and vibrant growth mindset environment.

To do list

- Make assemblies your own! Have a theme tune – create a buzz so learners look forward to them.
- Ask the children for feedback and ideas.
- Involve the teaching team in the planning and plan a cycle of two years of assemblies.
- Ask adults to stay to ensure the message is being communicated to everyone.
- Make them interactive – involve the children and have follow up activities for the week.
- Once your assemblies are established, ask the children to lead some of them.
- Take photos and have a 'growth mindset assembly of the week' board to display the main message.
- Use your social media to share your growth mindset assemblies with your stakeholders.

Chapter 6
Another motivational quote? Effective displays

I love displays! My creative mind buzzes when I think about how to display learning or a key message and I think there are many adults in schools who feel the same. The power that displays have is incredible – it is a portal to describe your learning culture to anyone who walks through the door and to send messages to children, staff, parents and additional adults. Displays should reflect the children as learners. Of course, children love to see their work on display, but every display should also convey the message that the school values effort, determination and the enjoyment of challenge. Some displays only value outcome. Unfortunately, this means that some children might never see their work on the wall. Displays that have a high level of interaction encourage children to engage with the school community because they know their input is valued. Allowing children to create or at least help create displays makes them feel they have made a real contribution to the learning environment. Some displays should value and highlight the processes of learning, rather than the outcome; all displays should reflect high aspirations, high expectations, process and contribution.

Thinking displays

The big question

Encourage children to contribute to a display about 'big questions' (see Chapter 1 for suggested questions). Display questions on the board surrounded by different responses. You could even leave some sticky notes next to the display for children and other visitors to write their response and add to the display. You can quickly create content by holding 'big question time' at the end of the school day and recording the responses.

The bookshelf

Displays don't always have to be boards on the wall. Create a display using a bookcase. Take some time to select high-quality texts for different ages groups. At my school I created a list of the books that could be found on the shelf, which helped maintain a high standard. We labelled it 'The Sharing Shelf'. Give children the option to borrow a text. In each book fasten an envelope to the inside cover containing slips of paper with questions for the children to fill in. You could change the question termly, some examples are: who would you recommend this book to? Who was your favourite character and why? If you were the author, how would you change the ending? Then, the next person to borrow the book can share these comments and add their own. Encourage your whole community to take part so children see a range of responses.

Planning circle

Challenge each class to create a display of their planning circle (see Chapter 1). Rotate this regularly to give each class the opportunity to create a display at some point in the school year. The topic of the planning circle should be the focus. Encourage the children to add photos and learning examples of the questions they had and how they have answered their enquiries. Learners are very proud to see how their learning builds up over time. If doing this with older children, you could also nominate a team of children to design the display, put it up or take photos for it – this ensures high engagement. A little light competition doesn't hurt either – which class has the best display? Maybe take a photo of each one and ask a governor to judge a yearly prize?

Fictional learner problem

Invent a problem that a child might have and display it. (You could even use a real problem you have heard from a child for really high engagement, but always keep it anonymous.) On the display pose the question, 'Can you help?'. This encourages other children to contribute ideas and help one another. To make it different and more exciting you could provide whiteboards, pens and pegs so they can hang their ideas up on a washing line. An example of a problem we displayed in my school was, 'I need help to master perimeter'. The ideas received were: watch a YouTube video, measure your garden to practise, draw a diagram to remind you, create perimeter Percy (apparently this is someone who only walks around edges!). You will be very surprised what the children come up with.

Say something

Use a stimulus as the main focus of the display. It could be a photograph, a picture or, in my school, I have used an open suitcase filled with interesting items. The more creative you are with your stimulus, the more engaged the children will be. Give the children a template to write a 100-word story based on the stimulus and then encourage them to display the stories. You could place a postbox nearby for children to post their stories in – empty it daily and put the stories up on the display. You could assign a time to do this during the school day. Alternatively, some children may want to write stories at home and bring them in because they are keen to have it displayed on the wall.

Ideas factory

Create a display with a large factory outline and allow children to contribute and display ideas for the school or for an event. Use this to involve the children in making whole-school decisions. For example: what colour should we paint our school and why? What do we need more of at school? What new clubs could we introduce? This shows that you value their opinion and also gives them an avenue to see what other children think.

Happy

Having optimistic thinking patterns improves resilience, so create boards of 'happy'! What makes the children happy? Create a display that reflects and showcases what it means to be happy. You can ask children to create work based around this theme and display it. You could also include photographs of happy times in school.

Weekly assembly focus

Create a display of the weekly assembly focus. This keeps the messages fresh in the mind of the children. You can create mini-tasks for them to complete during the week based on the theme. Use a postbox to collect responses or create a challenge they could present in assembly the following week.

Aspirational displays

Capture high expectations

A photograph says a thousand words. Take pictures of children going above and beyond. As a headteacher, I enjoy spending time walking around the school and taking photos of children who I have spotted doing something a little extra. At my school we annotated the photos and unveiled the display to the children as a surprise. They included: Molly picked up some litter; Ravi helped his teacher tidy up at break time, etc.

I can

Assign a time when you can discuss aspirations. I had a 'Who am I?' workshop and got the children to create butterflies that reflected on their goals. We displayed these in the main entrance to the school. It is often commented on by visitors. The children are so proud of the display that they are already planning the next one. I also gave them a copy of the photos of themselves holding their goals to put in their journals, so they could begin to plan how they could achieve their goals.

 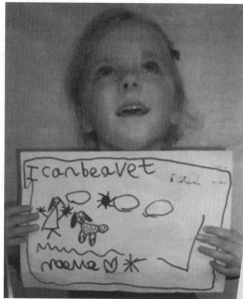

Make displays to raise aspirations and set goals – let the children lead

Where are they now?

Catch up with some past pupils – maybe Year 11s or 12s – and ask if they would like to visit the school or write a 'What I am doing now' article. Build a display around their responses. Anything you can display to show the children how past pupils have grown will be inspiring and, of course, include a picture of them when they were at the school. This display takes some planning but, once it is up and running, it has a great impact.

Growth mindset hero

Once the children are clear on the traits and behaviours of someone with a growth mindset, you can nominate a growth mindset hero. This could be a pupil at the school and you celebrate their learning behaviours. Alternatively, it could be someone in the media or a local person who has overcome something. If it someone in the school, include a photograph with them. (This is particularly effective if you can dress them up a hero too!) The children will aspire to be the hero!

Tries his best Tombear

Lots of primary schools have a bear that children in Reception and Key Stage 1 take turns to take home. Why not relate taking the bear home to your gowth mindset culture? Send home a book with the bear that children and parents can use to show the children trying their best at things throughout the week accompanied by the bear. It could include photos, writing or certificates, etc. You can display the bear's weekly travels or display him on social media as a #tryhisbesttombear.

The Power of Yet

This display builds on an activity introduced in Chapter 5 and you can find more ideas about how to involve parents and carers in this display in Chapter 8. Display pictures of everyone's 'yet'. You can add to this display at a later stage to show how children have achieved or made progress towards achieving their 'yet'.

Process displays

Goal timelines

This activity was introduced in Chapter 4, but why not make a display out of it? Having a goal is a trait of independent learners. Display the timeline of achieving a goal. This could be someone in the school, a parent or a famous figure.

Draft wall

These are similar to Working Walls, but they focus on writing. Display expected or exceeding statements and then explain what we mean when we talk about writing a draft of something – it is a first version of writing that we can go back and improve. Give the children time to create a draft piece of writing. Display their work on the wall. Then, throughout the week encourage the children to add their own work with ideas about how they can improve their writing. Allow them to use different coloured pens so that the feedback really stands out. As always, make sure the focus is on the 'how'!

Failures

Create a display showcasing famous failures to show children that some of the most valuable lessons are learnt as a result of failure. Search online and you will find many examples of famous figures who had to overcome failure. Add examples of failures experienced by the adults in school to the display too – this makes it more relatable. Encourage children to add failures they have overcome to the display. This display helps generate a culture where failures are celebrated not hidden.

Let me show you

Create a display that shows children how to do something in the style of a recipe. This could be how to make a paper aeroplane, how to draw a rabbit, how to write a story and much more. Use photographs to illustrate each step. At first you can show adults performing the steps, but later encourage children to share their knowledge of a process and provide a camera to take photos of each stage.

GRIT

Get ready it's time (GRIT)! Use this as a focus and encourage all stakeholders to bring in examples of when they needed GRIT! Ask children to bring in examples of hard work and parents to share challenges they have faced too. This is something parents love to get involved in. Examples I have seen in my school are: a pupil brought in her muddy races training plan, photo and medal; a governor brought in her accountancy course notes and certificate; a parent brought in a photo of her small gardening business and then a picture of her winning a prize at Chelsea Flower show. There are many things you could include, but create a display that really communicates that: hard work and effort = outcomes. Pure grit!

Improvement pen

Display a large sentence or short piece of writing and ask the learners to use the large improvement pen to interact with making it better. You can find brilliant large pens in most stationary shops.

The brain

Display a picture of a brain or, even better, get a class to make the brain on a large scale. Label parts of the brain so children can learn about the brain. Include messages that explain that it is an organ, but it behaves like a muscle, which means we have to exercise our brains through learning in order for our brains to grow.

Adults in school

Children love to see photographs of adults as babies or young children. Each week display an image of a baby or young child. Ask: who did this grow into? Give some clues of achievements or successes around the display to help the children figure out who it is. It encourages children to reflect that all adults were children once and are still growing and learning.

Motivation station

Transform a table or small board into a motivation station. Show the children strategies to motivate themselves and make these interactive so children can take something away too. Examples include: draw their dream, exercising, what can I achieve today cards, motivational quotes of the day, inspirational art on display.

Who inspires us?

I once sent my team the following message after a conference: 'How was your day? All ok? I met Derek Redmond – very inspirational I will say.' It was quickly picked up on and displayed. The children were then given the task of finding out who he was and why he was inspirational. It sparked lots of conversation and engagement from home and in school. Their findings were displayed. You can apply this theory to many people and ask the children why they are inspirational. Why do we admire their growth mindset? Get them to investigate and get motivated!

Headteacher's tea party

This is one of my favourite times in my school week. Each week I invite a child from each class to a tea party. We all share a special drink and a biscuit – there is a table cloth and everything to make it super special.

I regularly change the focus for the tea party. So, some weeks I might invite children who have overcome a great challenge, other weeks I might invite children who have tried something new or children who have taken great pride in the presentation of their work in their books, and so on. I love talking to the children about why they think they have been invited. The hard work and achievements of the children chosen that week is showcased on a special display. This models a growth mindset to other children and inspires them to receive an invitation.

Introduce a headteacher's tea party to keep expectations high

Summary

When children, adults and visitors walk round your school, displays can become wallpaper that no one takes any notice of. To help make people stop, read your displays and learn something from them, make the displays as child-led as possible. If the displays and environment shout the message of growth mindset and 'get involved', this will naturally translate in the attitudes of all the learners in the environment. Use your environment to create a buzz around growth mindset and it will embed into your culture, it will also remind the teachers and adults in the school constantly of the ethos you are creating for everyone. This support of the environment will help everyone when they are thinking about the feedback they give to learners in verbal and written feedback.

To do list

- Critically review the displays in your school as a team. What messages do they give out?
- Consider how interactive your displays are and could they be working harder for your culture?
- Delegate to members of the team to ensure interactive displays are maintained.
- Have high expectations of displays and this message will communicate to children who will rise to this when they interact.
- Review how child led your displays are. Get the learners involved.
- Include many stakeholders in your displays, parents, carers, governors, teachers, office staff and many more!

Chapter 7
Adult talk – why our language matters

Getting the 'adult talk' right in your school is a big challenge. It begins with developing the belief that everyone is capable of growth. This message should be embodied in educators' behaviour, their pedagogy and their language. Of course, there are many adults that already believe this and are, unconsciously, promoting growth mindset messages. However, there will also be adults in schools who do not believe this and have a fixed mindset themselves.

The first step is to evaluate your team's mindset. There are many online questionnaires you can use, or you can create your own using a model. (You may have already addressed this earlier in the project but, if you haven't yet, it is well worth doing.) The outcome of the questionnaire is to discover the overall mindset of the adults in your school. If you discover that many adults in your school already have a growth mindset, then you know they will be keen to learn and so you can immediately start working with them on the language they use and how they deliver feedback. However, if you conclude that the overall culture at your school is a fixed mindset, you will need to use a range of different methods to embed the mindset to ensure that all your adults are eager to learn themselves and see their own growth – which is what this chapter is all about.

Using some of the ideas below will ensure that the growth mindset message is being communicated by all the adults in your school and will ensure that the children in the school are very clear on the learning expectations. If everyone is communicating the same messages, everyone can feel confident in the growth mindset culture.

What language are we looking for?

Honest language is the best language (as long as you're not being rude and upsetting people). Growth mindset language is truthful, and, because of this, it actually helps us to improve something. As educators and parents, we often worry that telling the truth will damage self-esteem and create confidence problems. However, when was telling the truth such a bad thing? Children who continually hear fixed mindset messages – such as you're so clever, you're amazing at art, you're so good at maths – receive messages that they have no need for growth. If another adult or peer then tries to give them feedback, they often feel they have failed because they have never had to hear that they are less than perfect.

It is also important to remember that adults' communication with children starts in Reception, which is a key developmental time for language and communication. If you can get your growth mindset language right in the Early Years, you will reap the rewards in later years. Ensuring that there are spoken messages of growth mindset throughout the school will develop self-motivated and independent learners, which is what all schools hope for.

The difference with growth mindset language is that it shows children that there are expectations of growth and helps them to develop strategies of resilience, perseverance and problem-solving for themselves. In my experience, the majority of adults who work in primary schools are lovely and enthusiastic people – I like to call them WOW people! This is because I have seen so many occasions when children show the head or the teacher a piece of writing and receive an immediate WOW! And sometimes that's all it gets… How is the WOW actually helping them learn or become self-motivated learners? Ultimately, it's not! Now don't get me wrong, I am not a horrible dragon that doesn't enjoy looking at children's work – of course, I love pointing out the good things about their work. However, my golden rule is that learning doesn't end, so don't let the feedback end. I keep this phrase in my head all the time when talking to children and to adults. If I could, I would have it on a t-shirt because it always reminds me to say something that will help the child to move forward.

The learning doesn't end…

So, when a child shows you a piece of work they are clearly very proud of try not to just say, 'WOW'; instead, say, 'Can you tell me a about it?'. I am not suggesting that you shoot them down in flames but by asking learners to explain their processes, decisions and thoughts, you are making them more aware of 'how' they did something. Over time, it will become natural for them to think about how to improve their work. Put the emphasis on them to tell you what processes they have been through, what they think is good and what has challenged them. Here are some other questions to get you started:

- Can you tell me which part challenged you?
- How could you make it harder?
- Why did you choose…?
- What made you use that word?
- How would you explain to your friend how to do this task?
- Is it your best effort? How do you know?
- What would you do differently next time?

Always give feedback – no matter how amazing you think the work is. What advice could you give to help the learner improve it? Make sure they explain it, evaluate it and consider the next step.

Reduced to nagging about effort...

Good growth mindset language is not just about telling children to try harder – that is just nagging and is not constructive. Why should they try harder? What are they trying to achieve? How will they achieve it? What skills to they need to develop? Some of the language used in schools is focused around GRIT (see Chapter 3) and trying hard but it is important to remember that this is only one aspect of a growth mindset. All aspects should be addressed in language. The building blocks of getting it right are developing the learner's skills in reflecting on their own learning journey. So, what kind of language SHOULD we be using?

Good mistakes

Get into the habit of asking learners to identify mistakes. As discussed in the previous chapters, make talking about mistakes 'normal' language. 'Mistakes are how we learn' is a stock phase in a growth mindset school.

Reframing

Reframe language in the classroom continually. There are many display resources that demonstrate this. 'I can't do it...' becomes 'Can you think of what might help you to do it?' Model reframing language and questions and ask children to think about the words they have used and see if they can find a reframed phrase.

Growth mindset mottos

The children at my school can almost predict what I will say in certain situations – we even have some of our key growth mindset phrases printed on our books. Get into the habit of using growth mindset phrases as part of your culture: use them around children, staff, parents and governors, so everyone understands the message. In order for all your adults to 'get on board' with growth mindset language, they need to hear it in action regularly. This sounds obvious, but in order to embed growth mindset every member of the team has to model it and not just in front of the children. If the team don't believe that the SLT believe in growth mindset, they won't even give it a chance. As a team, you can create your own bank of mottos and phrases to use and they will naturally evolve. In the meantime, here are some phrases you could try:

- Everything is hard until it's easy.
- That's too easy and we weren't made for easy.
- If it's a challenge, you're learning.
- Mistakes are how we learn.
- Failures happen everywhere and to everyone. What can we do next?
- Practice makes sense.
- Your brain needs some exercise – work out!

Record the language you use

Once you are clear as a team on the difference between fixed mindset and growth mindset language, create some opportunities to peer observe and give each other some feedback. Often, we don't realise what we say: for example, I did not realise how many times I said 'absolutely' until it was pointed out to me. I still say it a lot, but I am weaning myself off. Of course, staff can give each other feedback in a non-formal way, but here are some useful ways to record the language you use and assess what kind of messages it is giving children.

Observation tally chart

Snapshot observation focusing on feedback and language used is very effective: you can easily monitor this by drawing a chart with two columns and a simple tally for fixed and growth statements. You can make additional notes of what was actually said to remind you when you discuss it with the teacher afterwards. Then, as a professional partnership, discuss your findings – this can then lead to a staff workshop where you can collate good growth mindset phases.

Filming

Most school staff panic when the idea of filming is mentioned, but it is an effective way to observe the language used in the school. Rather than a member of SLT doing the filming, ask some older children to conduct a filming study of the teaching language and to evaluate whether it promotes a growth mindset. Ask them to spend time with all adults. This also supports the computing curriculum.

Language walls

Once you have demonstrated, evaluated and modelled your language, begin to ask your team to contribute to a working wall of language phrases. What works? What questions work well in different situations? Encourage all adults to complete a speech bubble giving some context and what language they used to promote growth mindset – this will be a good learning tool for less confident staff.

Feedback

Questioning

All practitioners use questions in teaching, so evaluate the depth of your questioning in the classroom regularly. Get into the habit of questioning everything the children in your class do. Put a huge question mark up in your classroom as a prompt for any time during the lesson. Ask questions about the learning and ask the children to ask each other questions. They will get used to the process of explaining their choices and how they reached conclusions. The outcome of this is that it encourages them to evaluate their own learning.

Information, behaviour and the future

When giving learners verbal feedback about their work, use the model above. Give learners information about their learning – what learning behaviour does it show? Then, describe the behaviour used to achieve the learning. Finally, give feedback for the future – where can they go next? If you continually structure your feedback using this framework, it will be more effective because it will help children to develop. Here are some models you could adapt:

- You need to… Next time… Did you challenge yourself here?
- That's a good painting – what would you do next time with the colours?
- If you had more time, how would you develop it?
- I like your rocket model – what could you do to make it even better?
- Explain your workings on your fractions problem; do you think you should try a harder one now?

You can teach this model to learners, too. Have a grid up in the classroom with the following headers: Information, Behaviour and Future. Ask them to evaluate the feedback they are given by adults by putting it into the appropriate column. Ask them to highlight feedback that they think fulfils growth mindset.

Marking – the ultimate feedback

Marking is a golden opportunity to review whether the feedback you give your learners demonstrates a fixed or a growth mindset.

In my career I have often found that when you take the books away over the weekend and return them on Monday, younger children have completely forgotten what the learning objectives were and, in order for them to even begin to improve, they almost have to relearn the task. To make sure that feedback is always productive at my school we have introduced live feedback initiative. This means that children know what they are doing well and what they need to improve on immediately.

In live marking, books are marked within the lesson by an adult. Our live marking initiative centres around highlighter pens. Each colour represents a different element of feedback. For example, blue marks grammar. The colour code is consistent across the school, which means that the children can easily decipher their feedback. It also means that all adults in the school can feedback on children's learning. This includes me too – I often wander into classrooms with my highlighters ready.

This type of feedback eliminates time consuming comments such as 'I enjoyed your story', 'I loved your sentences' and 'Well done'. Children do need to hear affirmations, but these can be given verbally. Writing these comments takes time and we need to ask ourselves: does our marking progress learning? Does it promote a growth mindset?

I actually stop teachers now if I see them with carrier bags of books. Most have got their live marking down to a fine art and it eliminates the need to spend hours writing comments. As a team we have developed grow stickers that ensure all learners are being treated as individuals and being challenged continually, which is what I am going to talk about next.

Use stickers for live feedback

Why use stickers?

- They are quick and easy to make. We design our own and regularly change them. The staff give new ideas for stickers all the time. This also means the team feels involved.

- It is immediate feedback and live – it happens at the time of learning.

- There is a limited space, so it doesn't encourage endless words – just feedback and next step.

- You can personalise learning quickly. The adults use these in the classroom and they are personalised for each learner, depending on where they are in their learning.

- It is easy to see if the next step has been addressed – I have seen so many books where the next step is capital letters and it has been the same next step for a term.

We have developed many different stickers and are always developing more examples. These include: Too many ticks, Now try this, Improve the sentence, Find the mistake and fix it, Super challenge, etc. We also use growing writer stickers. These have three bullets points for improvements and the children are encouraged to refer to them in their next piece of work. The important thing is to keep stickers simple – this makes for effective, clear feedback that both the child and teacher can reflect on to make sure the next step has been addressed.

Every adult's language counts

It is important that all adults in the school are aware of how they communicate and feedback to children. Try these techniques to bring growth mindset language to their attention:

- Invite the children to post 'growth' feedback they have received at lunchtime.
- Have a growth and fixed mindset piggy bank in the office – post tokens when anyone hears either during the day.
- Publish a growth mindset quote of the week in your newsletter.
- Use social media to film growth mindset language examples.
- Get into the habit of giving each other feedback on processes throughout the school and create an improvement book for all staff.
- Involve every member of staff in everything where possible. Office staff and midday assistants can often feel isolated from school life, so make sure they are a part of it where possible. For example, invite them to be judges at the school talent competition.

Ensure you are creating a culture that welcomes feedback and goes a little further than the annual parent questionnaire. Take any opportunity to receive ideas and feedback from all your stakeholders.

- After parent assemblies or gatherings ask a question: what do you like about our school? What clubs would you like to see?
- Create a celebration or a growth tree. Ask visitors to give you feedback on their visit and any advice to improve.
- Use social media to encourage positive feedback.
- Invite parents to observe your school parliament or council.
- Have comments forms at reception for parents/carers to post.
- Have idea speech bubbles available for adults to make suggestions.

Ensure you are promoting that as an organisation you listen!

Celebrate and engage with the community

University challenge

Encourage your team to share their passions with the children. One way of doing this is to create 'courses' reflecting the passions of your staff that the children can sign up to for a fixed period of time. Then, nominate a time where children can go to their chosen course. Example of different courses include: crochet, gardening, mechanics, origami, cooking. The list is endless! The key for success with this is that the adults in the school have suggested the courses – nothing makes people enjoy learning more than teaching something they love and seeing others getting enjoyment from it. If nothing else, the children have learnt some fantastic key skills in a way where the focus is on the learning. How do we learn? What helps us to learn? Ask your team to honestly reflect on these questions after their courses and this can begin your discussions about language.

Summary

To ensure the development of a growth mindset you need to evaluate the language that adults in the school use when communicating with children, in both verbally and written feedback. All feedback should aim to help children make progress – it shouldn't just be done to tick a box. The importance of effective feedback can be seen in the progress and learning attitudes of children. A school with prompt, constructive feedback will ensure rapid progress, support independent learners and hopefully ensure that marking workload is reduced as all feedback is relevant and useful.

Parents and carers can also help embed a growth mindset through the messages they give learners at home. The next chapter looks at how to involve them and give them the tools to help embed the growth mindset message further.

To do list

- Review your marking policy. Does it allow for live marking? Or is all marking taking place away from the learner? Are they receiving delayed feedback?
- How does the school support teacher's workload to enable more live feedback?
- Evaluate the language and mindset of all adults. Develop an action plan to improve the messages given to children through the communications.
- Involve all adults in the process of evaluating the language used in the school.
- Model continually the language you want your team to use towards learners in your new culture.
- Ensure you are a culture that accepts and listens to feedback yourself; go beyond your annual parent survey.

Chapter 8
The power of the parent

All educational settings know the importance of parental engagement in improving the outcomes for all children. Equally, they also know that it is not always easy to engage parents and carers in today's hectic world. In order for a growth mindset culture to develop, all stakeholders should be aware and understand the key values and ideas, as well as being aware of their own influence on its success.

The first step is to show how a growth mindset is relevant to them; if they feel that it is an alien concept they won't engage. Most parents and carers will endeavour to make time to come into school if they feel they are influencing or impacting on their child's learning and development, so take advantage of this and run a session to explain the principles of a growth mindset and inform them of any changes you will be making in your setting to accommodate it. After you have sowed the seeds, there are many ways to develop their mindset with regular communication.

Create opportunities for parents to embrace the growth mindset culture themselves so they can support at home with healthy learning messages. This is important because, considering busy lifestyles, it is not always possible for parents to keep coming into school. There are many ideas in this chapter to help engagement. Adapt them for your audience, if you have low parental uptake to invites into school, use social media to spread your message using video links. Make your engagement work for your audience.

Challenge day

A great way to introduce the idea of a growth mindset to parents is to tag your first session onto a child-led activity. Plan a challenge day in school where the emphasis is on activities that are focused on problem-solving. STEM activities are great for this and so are maths problems where learners need to work in teams.

At the end of the school day, set up the classrooms so parents can visit their children and see what they have been doing and chat to them about their day. Following this, invite them to the hall and give a short presentation on growth mindset. This is your first opportunity to explain how important it is and what you as a school are doing to embed it. Just compare a growth mindset with a fixed mindset in this session – this might be the first time parents have of heard of it, so it is best to keep it simple. Videos are great starting points and there are many on YouTube that cover the basic concept. Introduce parents to the reasons why you, as a school, think it is key for the learners to develop their growth mindset.

Workshop

Everyone gets a little fed up of being talked at, so an active workshop is a great way to engage parents and careers. It gets them 'doing' and it is a great way to get the message across. All the training or information sessions I lead always include some activities – people remember these things far more than a PowerPoint presentation and being talked at. Make it memorable! Recently I held a workshop and afterwards a parent said to me, 'It's all just clicked into place for me!'.

Below is a tried-and-tested workshop format that engages parents and gives them ideas on how they can support a growth mindset for the learners in their lives. It will cover:

1. Lead by example
2. Call off the rescue mission
3. Why is failure such a bad thing?
4. Change your words
5. The power of yet.

1. Lead by example

Introduce this concept by asking your audience to fold an A3 piece of paper in half and on one half draw a self-portrait. Stop – this is the moment you will hear a room of uncomfortable adults saying things like, 'I can't draw', 'I know it won't look like me'. In one workshop I led, we actually held a phrase bingo and pulled out phrases we thought we might hear and asked them if they had said it. This highlighted to the adults that what they say reflects their mindset. At the thought of doing something hard, they are immediately worried about failing. After some considerable giggling, all the adults drew a picture of themselves. Then one of the teachers gave them some feedback on their drawings and then gave a five-minute lesson on how to draw a face.

Hold active workshops for parents and carers to begin to engage with growth mindset

After this short session, adults were able to describe what they thought was good about their drawing. Of course, they didn't think they could draw like an artist, but they were pleased with the improvement. This activity opened up a discussion about how, as adults, we are modelling that we are learners too and that we need to show children that we are open to feedback and need to embrace challenges even if we think we can't do them.

The same activity works with many different tasks not just drawing a portrait, such as origami, Suduko and fractions.

2. Call off the rescue mission

This is an opportunity to talk about helicopter parenting. We all want our children to be successful, but by constantly hovering it means that they don't feel failure, which actually embeds a fixed mindset. Helicopter parents take too much responsibility for their children's successes and failures and typically become too involved in their learning experiences – this can lead to children not taking responsibility for their own learning. In the workshop, run a couple of activities to highlight this to parents.

Start by getting parents to complete this online survey about helicopter parenting on laptops or iPads® if you have them: BBC iWonder – Am I a helicopter parent?

After they have completed the survey, ask them to anonymously write on a piece of paper if they have done something that could be considered an example of 'helicopter parenting'. Collect these up, read a few out and ask parents what messages these examples give to the children about their learning. Here are some of the responses we received:

- 'I telephoned my child's teacher and asked her to let him off the spelling test as he hadn't prepared for it.' (Parent of a Year 3 child)
- 'I did my daughter's art project for her while she was asleep.' (Parent of a Year 5 child)
- 'I kept my son off football training because I knew he wasn't going to get picked for the team.' (Parent of a Year 6 child)

The above are all real responses and they give a real insight into how some parents feel. We then discussed what would have happened if the parent had not done this. This highlighted to many parents how they fear their children's failure. I asked them to consider whether allowing their child to fail might actually have been a good lesson for them that they will remember in future. By doing the exercise it highlighted to many that, although we realise all these things come from a loving place, they are actually terminating a growth mindset in children because they protect them from failure. As a group, we talked about how to build up resilience.

This is a good point in the workshop to bring in techniques on how to deal with inevitable failures in all our lives and how we deal with them as parents. Get the parents to work on tables and take some of these scenarios and discuss what they could do that would help them develop a better mindset. At the workshop I led, parents were honest about many situations and agreed that actually giving the children tools to succeed on their own was better than overprotecting them. The parent with the phone call about the spelling test, for example, agreed that a better way of dealing with the situation would be to encourage her son to face the consequences of having not prepared. The key to a successful workshop is giving your audience the tools to find the answers themselves.

3. Why is failure such a bad thing?

Use this question as a platform to talk about homework or school competitions – it will make them laugh if nothing else! Talk about situations. For example, describe the entries received in something like the Easter bonnet competition, where teachers are presented with beautiful, elaborate entries and are supposed to believe that a five-year-old produced it. I like to show two examples of a child's artwork at this point: one that has been heavily guided by an adult and another that is independent and child-led. Ask the parents to consider the 'process' of learning rather than the outcome. What can we learn from failure and is it such a bad thing?

4. Change your words

At one workshop I led, I showed a video of myself praising a child where I went completely bonkers over a piece of writing, but there was no constructive feedback that could help the child's learning move on. I asked the parents what they thought about this. I received mixed reviews: some thought it was lovely and others thought it was a little over-the-top. Of course, it was over-the-top on purpose, but it's not uncommon. I explained how giving feedback that is just praise told the child that they were finished and there was no more learning to be done.

Then, show another video with the same praise but include a clear growth mindset phase, such as 'I like the adjectives you have used – have you thought about any different ones you could have used?'.

In this part of the workshop, it is essential to give the parents ideas of what they can say. Give a handout of ideas about how to use praise effectively. Explain that telling your child that they are clever, that you are proud of their 'A' or that they are really talented is not useful when developing a growth mindset.

- 'Wow, great result. You clearly tired really hard and your extra effort has paid off.'
- 'A good start, let's try something even more challenging to help you improve.'
- 'The amount of work and effort you put into being a musician/athlete/mathematician has helped you to make excellent progress.'
- 'You really studied hard for your English test and your improvement shows, good idea to read the material and then test yourself, that really worked.'
- 'You haven't quite mastered that topic in maths yet, talk to your teacher, complete some more practice questions and you will improve further.'

---

5. The power of yet

I love to show the Sesame Street™ song, the 'Power of Yet', at this point – who can resist Elmo? It is easily found on YouTube. It is key that the parents challenge their child's fixed mindset with the 'yet' word: 'I can't do fractions in maths… yet'. At this point of the workshop ask the audience, 'What is your 'yet' at this moment in life?'. Ask them to record it, chat about it and then invite them to have their photo taken holding their 'yet'. This is useful as it highlights how they can support their child's 'yet', but also how they can model their continued growth as an individual. You can then use the photos to create a display to show the learners in the school, modelling that adults have 'yets' too – we are all on a journey of improvement!

Engage everyone in the message of growth mindset

Social media

In today's modern world no one can ignore social media and, as long as it's monitored, it can be a very effective tool to communicate positive messages about the learning culture of your school. Most schools engage with social media now. I like Twitter, as it feels more interactive and there is less gossip and more positivity. When setting up any social media group for your school, make sure your policy is airtight and you have permission from parents and carers to share photos. All staff need to be aware of any children whose parents or carers have not given permission. At my school we have a staff of 40 and only three members of staff (two of which are SLT) contribute to the Twitter feed. Other members of the team know they can make them aware of any photos they think would be good on the feed and they will be put on as long as they are promoting positive messages. It is tempting to allow lots of staff to have access to your Twitter feed, but, when you are using it to promote certain messages, I would recommend assigning a specific person to ensure the messages consistently promote your culture.

Once you have all your boundaries and policies in place, it is a great platform to promote your growth mindset message. In your feed include lots of examples of effort-related successes. Keep referring to items where challenges have been faced or where children have experienced hard work. Daily life at school is good to include on your feed as well, as it gives the community an insight into what a school day looks like.

Once you have established your social media, you can encourage parents and carers to engage with it. Introduce hashtags that celebrate a growth mindset attitude. Here are some successful ones we have sent home to parents as 'home learning'. We introduced these in assemblies or set them as challenges on the weekly newsletters. They have also been sent home in reading records for an extra challenge at home.

- #challenge
- #sweatybrow
- #allbymyself
- #whoopsmistake
- #fail
- #mylearning

Invite them in to share their experiences

Lots of parents love to be involved in school life. Send out a letter asking if they have a growth mindset experience they would like to share: would they like to talk to the children about something they have overcome or mistakes they have made? I had one parent who talked openly about her dyslexia and how she found ways to overcome it. I also had a dad who came in and talked about how he trained to run the London Marathon.

A place of learning for everyone

To effectively promote a growth mindset message, you need to include all your stakeholders in learning – it is important that everyone knows we never stop learning and that is an important message for the children too. Contact local colleges and see if they would like to run a short course for parents at the school. Local health authorities often run parenting courses, so invite them in. You will have a range of skills within your teaching staff, so utilise this. We ran a knitting club for parents run by an LSA. Getting parents and carers involved in the learning journey is the important message. Then, display pictures of this learning for the children to see – it is a powerful message that we are all learning and improving all the time.

Summary

Engaging parents and carers in the school community is part of embedding the growth mindset. The messages of growth mindset are not just for educational settings, they are for life and once you begin to explore this with parents they will begin to make links with their own experiences. Involving adults in practical activities ensures it stays with them and involves them in the process in truly embedding the new growth mindset culture.

To do list

- Review your communications with parents – does it promote growth mindset?
- Design an interactive workshop that teaches them the message of growth mindset.
- Use social media to engage them in challenge and learning.
- Invite them in to see the children solving open-ended problems and challenges.
- Involve them in passing the message on to the children and to share their experiences.
- Make the school a learning place for all – run workshops or classes for parents to enjoy learning themselves.

Chapter 9

Impact – what does it look like now?

So, you have championed the philosophy of a growth mindset and you've implemented it into your school culture. The displays are interactive, child-led learning is taking place, learners are feeling empowered and there is a clear feeling of independence in learners. You know that all your hard work has had impact, but how do you show the impact and how do you maintain it in the school? That's what this final chapter is all about.

Assessing the culture

As I mentioned at the beginning, the before and after is key to any project, so make sure that your growth mindset objectives established what the situation was like before, so you can easily see how it has changed after. Look back at the objectives you made at the beginning and think about how you would assess whether you have achieved them.

Mindset questionnaires: Pupils, staff and school

One way that you can assess if you've met your objectives is by using mindset questionnaires. The answers will inform you of the areas still to work on and show the progress you have made. You can find many templates online, but it is key you decide on the questions you ask based on your school and your objectives. At my school, for example, we had groups of children who wouldn't try when they found things challenging – they had lost their confidence. This was our starting point, so it influenced our impact questions. Agree as a team what your focus is. Of course, this can change and develop as you work through and develop your culture. Make sure you re-ask the questions you began with before the school embarked on the growth mindset journey too. Draw up a scale from one to five for respondents to mark their answer and agree what the results would look like at each point on the scale. You could use an online questionnaire tool to collate the results for you. Keep your questions simple:

*   How independent are our learners?
*   How child-led is the learning?

- How resilient are our learners?
- How much do our children know about how to learn? The process?

Learning walks

Often learning walks are seen as 'fluffy'! However, I think they are great. At my school, I walk around the school every day, sometimes for ten minutes, sometimes longer. On a learning walk you can feel the learning environment and you will quickly establish key pointers to look for when assessing the impact of the developing culture. Build an observation list with the rest of your SLT, but don't take it with you – you don't need to. Walk around the school with your team or alone and then review your list when you return. Think of the walk as a snapshot of your environment. Once you have produced an observation list for your school, share it and get others to share any lists they have or add anything they think should be on your list. People to share it with could include: teachers, the office staff and governors.

Here are some examples of observation criteria to assess on your learning walk. For every statement, show evidence. And if there isn't any evidence, this will help you identify what your next step for the culture should be. Make it about your setting – personalise it.

- Learners are very engaged in learning.
- Learners make their own choices about learning.
- Growth mindset language is used regularly.
- Feedback is welcomed and useful.
- The school is interactive and welcomes views of all.
- Learners feel empowered.

Questionnaires: Parents

Include growth mindset questions in your parent questionnaire. Highlight it as an important part of your feedback process. Here are some examples of questions you could ask:

- Is your child resilient at school?
- How does your child react to making mistakes?
- Do you think the feedback given to your child is valuable to progress?
- How does your child feel about learning?

Pupil's voice

Don't underestimate the voice of the learner when measuring impact. We ask learners for their opinion about lots of issues through the school council, but do we ask them how they feel about learning and the environment? Talk to your learners regularly about their learning behaviours, barriers and self-esteem. Set up a learner's focus group specifically for this purpose. Invite their opinions as children are always honest!

Progress and attainment data

Data – some of us love it, some of us hate it, but it cannot be ignored. It is useful to track a percentage of children before and after the project and look for impact. Pupil progress is tracked continually, but is the culture shift making a difference to progress of groups? If you identified a group of learners who didn't work independently very frequently, see if you can see a change in their attainment data as this will signal the impact of your new culture.

How to keep the culture alive?

Make a growth mindset less of a 'new thing' and more of a 'this is just what we do here'. The more you make the growth mindset culture the property of everyone, the less it relies on one person championing it. We can all remember projects that worked really well because Mr X was so passionate about it, but when he left the project slowly faded away. To make the culture of growth mindset stick it has to be embedded in what everyone does and that takes time. Even once you think it's comfortably in place, keep it as a focus on staff meeting agendas, governor's meetings, make sure your staffroom displays are up to date, have a gowth mindset notice board with the latest observations and achievements on, etc. Delegate the responsibility of promoting its message amongst the team so it belongs to everyone: let someone take charge of assemblies, another team member could be responsible for a single display.

Performance management

Make growth mindset a part of everyone's PMR. You'd be surprised how powerful this is at ensuring that all staff are contributing and working hard to achieve it. This also demonstrates to staff the importance you as a school have placed on it. Objectives could be: to give live feedback to children to ensure progress in that lesson, facilitate child-led learning in the planning of lessons or create opportunities for children to reflect on learning regularly.

School improvement plan: The journey wall

Make growth mindset part of your school improvement plan (SIP) and include the objectives that you are working towards. Some schools write their SIP yearly, but I like to write it termly to show rapid improvement and change. Create a journey wall – this is a working wall for staff. Have your objectives up on the wall and show how staff have contributed to them, this shows staff that their contribution counts. Regularly ask for contributions to the wall – this could be in the form of photos, sticky notes, planning or any form! Everyone can contribute to the ongoing development of culture. At my school a wonderful sticky note was put up on the journey wall by a member of the office team. It read, 'Child X told me he was getting better at maths… I told him I was getting better at cooking!',

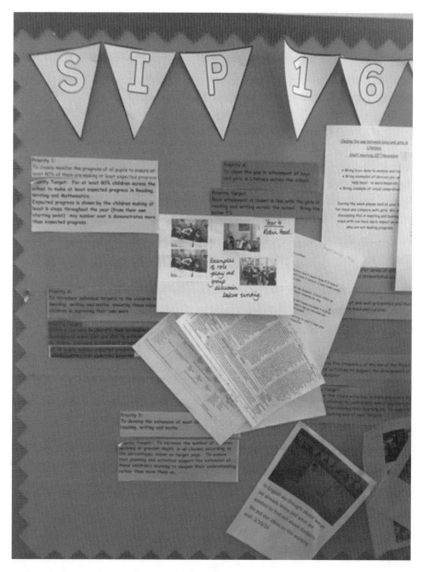

Encourage the whole team to contribute to the learning and development of the growth mindset culture in the school

Reflect, review and reinforce

The best learners reflect on everything they do. Then, they adapt it, review it and make changes to be better. Model this process continually in your school and ask the team to help. If everyone gets on board with looking at how things are working and what you are achieving, it will keep it in focus. Here are some suggestions for how to do this:

- Hold staff workshops on methods of feedback and peer review each other.
- Ask for opinions on the question of the week in the staffroom. Do our classrooms show children leading learning? How?

- Go on a mass learning walk.
- Have a very large communal journal for all team members to reflect on different areas of growth mindset. Ask about working walls? Are they working?
- Assess workload regularly. Is your team working effectively or wasting time on paperwork that doesn't need to be done? How can you change it?

Celebrate

Ensure you are celebrating your achievements – the small ones as well! Continually show people in the school and school community how you are teaching the children, share everything that shows process. Model to all how effort counts and how much you value it.

To do list

- Include growth mindset objectives in the school improvement plan.
- Develop personalised questionnaires to measure before and after impact.
- Use groups of children's data to track progress and attainment.
- Celebrate everything!
- Make reflection and review common place.
- Create a school where ownership is valued and ask everyone to show and be proud of how they have contributed to the culture.
- Include growth mindset in performance management objectives.
- Keep it at the top of agendas!

Bibliography

Professional development

Dix, P. (2017), *When the Adults Change, Everything Changes: Seismic Shifts in School Behaviour*. Carmarthen: Independent Thinking Press.

Dweck, C. (2017), *Mindset: Changing The Way You Think to Fulfil Your Potential* (Updated Edition). London: Robinson.

Syed, M. (2010), *Bounce: The Myth of Talent and the Power of Practice*. London: Fourth Estate.

Story books

Andres, G. and Parker-Rees, G. (2014), *Giraffes Can't Dance*. London: Orchard Books.

Bright, R. and Field, J. (2015), *The Lion Inside*. London: Orchard Books.

Daywalt, D. and Jeffers, O. (2014), *The Day the Crayons Quit*. London: HarperCollins.

Freeman, C. and Cort, B. (2007), *Aliens Love Underpants*. London: Simon and Schuster.

Könnecke, O. (2015), *You Can Do It, Bert!*. Wellington: Gecko Press.

Pett, M. and Rubinstein, G. (2012), *The Girl Who Never Made Mistakes*. Chicago: Sourcebooks Jabberwocky.

Reynolds, P. H. (2005), *Ish*. London: Walker.

Reynolds, P. H. (2004), *The Dot*. London: Walker.

Saltzburg, B. (2010), *Beautiful OOPS*. New York: Workman Publishing.

Video resources

Type the following into YouTube:

'Power of Yet' Sesame Street™

Austin's Butterfly

SOAR: a short movie

Other online resources

Type the following into Google or your preferred search engine:

BBC iWonder – Am I a helicopter parent?